THE SEVEN DIMENSIONS OF BRANDING

THE SEVEN DIMENSIONS OF BRANDING

BRAND BUILDING FROM THE AFRICAN PERSPECTIVE.

MUYIWA KAYODE

authorHOUSE®

AuthorHouse™
1663 Liberty Drive
Bloomington, IN 47403
www.authorhouse.com
Phone: 1-800-839-8640

First published by AuthorHouse   08/25/2011

ISBN: 978-1-4634-3429-8 (sc)
ISBN: 978-1-4634-3428-1 (hc)
ISBN: 978-1-4634-3427-4 (ebk)

Library of Congress Control Number: 2011915368

Printed in the United States of America

OUTLINE

AKNOWLEDGMENTS

I owe a world of gratitude to several people for their influence and contributions over the four years it took to put this book together. Some of them made their contributions during brief moments of intellectual discourse, while others had a more profound impact. My friend and business partner, Kunle Ajose stands out. Right from the start while trying to determine a conceptual approach, an appropriate title and eventually the 'right' cover design and author photograph, he was a constant influence all the way.

My Chairman, Akin Kekere-Ekun was a rock solid pillar of support, especially at a time we audaciously decided to venture into the 'unknown', by becoming Nigeria's Premier Brand Management Consultancy. His support of my two courses at Harvard Business School was fundamental in shaping the thinking expressed in this book. I equally thank Falalu Bello, Remi Kolarinwa, Segun Fowora, Sunil Mahbubani, Dada Ajai-Ikhile, Jamilu Jibrin, Bashir el Rufai and Lamis Dikko.

My gratitude goes to Akinsola Akinfemiwa, one of the quintessential bankers that shaped the modern landscape of Nigerian banking and provided the platform on which our brand management practice thrived. The Lady I describe as Nigeria's Lady Captain of Industry, Stella Okoli, foremost industrialist and brand champion has been a constant source of inspiration while her company provided some of the experiences that enriched this book. And of course Nigeria's digital entrepreneur Leo Stan Ekeh, who says 'The story of Zinox, Nigeria's first internationally certified brand of computer, would not be complete without USP', for giving us the opportunity to help conceive and deliver ZINOX, now a fast growing international brand with the potential to become a truly global brand out of Africa.

My friend and Harvard course mate Jamie Pleasant was wonderfully supportive all the way while I owe a lot to insightful perspectives provided by faculty members Youngme Moon, David Godes and Kashturi Rangan.

Immense gratitude goes to Darl Uzu, who signed the first cheque USP received as a company and demanded uncompromising standards in his quest to build a leading real estate brand. Right from those early days, the challenges thrust upon me and my team by the numerous clients we worked with provided the basis for some of the arguments advanced in this book. By this token, I thank Lawrence Osa Afiana, Erastus Akingbola, Mike Chukwu, Tony Elumelu, Ifie Sekibo, Frank Aigbogun, Rasheed Sarumi, Wole Adeyegbe, Otunba Remi Abdul, Segun Awolowo, Bello Maccido, Bassey Ndem, Segun Ologunleko, Ola Rahman and Muhtar Bakare.

I also thank Aniekan Umanah, Inyang Etido, Mohammed Kari, Bala Zakariya'u, Abraham Igbehinadara, Onyeka Onyeibor, and Alex Okoh. I thank Osarentin Odaro for guiding me with professional insights at certain times along the way; Udeme Ufot, Julia Oku and Lolu Akinwunmi for imparting knowledge and experience; Akin Adeoya, Sola Salako and Joko Okupe for sharing "the brand vision". My gratitude also goes to Lere Baale and Stanley Okocha. I thank Olawunmi Ajibola for proofreading and all my colleagues at USP, past and present.

My lifelong vision of becoming an author has been wholeheartedly supported by my family, Hetty, Omololu and Adanma to whom I owe my brand identity!

And most importantly, I thank the Almighty for the vision and the means to translate it to reality.

PREFACE

In March 2003, USP, the advertising company I co-founded with two friends and colleagues caused a stir in the marketing communications sphere, by announcing its withdrawal from the Association of Advertising Agencies of Nigeria, AAAN. As soon as the news was reported, I received a congratulatory text message from a leading PR practitioner and a former senior colleague during my days as a journalist, Taiwo Obe. He was just one of quite a number of professionals who felt the advertising body was mired in the past, and not in tune with the yearnings of its members.

Since such a move was at the time "unheard of", the advertising body was at a loss on how to respond. I received a call from the President of AAAN at the time, Bola Thomas, who asked why we made such a move during her time in office. A few days later, I received a letter from the Advertising Practitioners Council, APCON the body mandated by law to regulate the practice of advertising in Nigeria. The letter reminded us that we needed to belong to a professional body in order to practice advertising, but the body could not pursue the matter further since it was beyond what it was mandated to do. USP's position was that it had repositioned as a brand management consultancy and continued membership of AAAN would not support this new positioning. This set the stage for what later became a topical issue in the industry and a cold war between advertising agencies and the emerging brand consultancies. The advertising establishment insisted that there was no difference between advertising and brand management. Most of them promptly changed their client service departments to "Brand Management Department". Their client service managers started going by the title of brand managers. They had thus commenced a campaign aimed at confusing unsuspecting clients regarding the distinction between advertising and branding. While there were many who clearly did not understand the distinction, there were those who felt "threatened" by the imminent emergence of a new category with a more compelling value proposition. Some even argued that brand management was a part of marketing communications, hence the creation of brand management departments within their advertising agencies.

It is easy to understand this confused reaction. Clients were becoming disenchanted with traditional advertising agencies. They wanted much more than traditional advertising could offer but they were not getting it. Their businesses required deep strategic thinking, which the agencies were not structured to provide. Where a product needed a strong value proposition and excellent packaging, they simply rushed it to market and launched expensive advertising. With the more strategic and holistic approach of brand consulting, we were able to guide clients through the various stages of the branding process, before the stage at which they could go to market with a compelling value proposition.

In a country where the leading agencies are affiliates of global advertising networks and the leading brands are owned by multinationals, there were limited opportunities for such agencies to develop competencies in strategic brand management. An entrepreneur trying to create an original brand in such an environment would require much more than mere advertising. Brand consultants have since emerged to meet this need while traditional advertising has not lost its relevance in the process of building and managing brands.

Given the peculiarities and the social complexity of the African continent, managers of global brands often discover, sometimes at great cost that their strategies need a bit of tweaking for them to succeed in this vast emerging market. *The Seven Dimensions of Branding* examines the universal principles of branding from the perspective of a developing economy in Africa's most populous nation. The book shows that those principles may be universal, but their application is not.

THE FIRST DIMENSION

"

In articulating a sound vision, an important question to ask is "Why do we exist?" It is common to make the mistake of answering this question with "To make money". This is based on the general belief that every business exists purely for profit. While profit is essential for the survival of the business, it must never be regarded as the company's reason for being.

"

BRAND VISION

Most corporations have Vision and Mission Statements. However, do these statements have a positive impact on corporate and employee behavior? This question has prompted marketing scholars to examine the ability of companies to establish a connection between their vision and mission statements and employee behavior.

The process of articulating a vision and mission statement seems simple and straightforward. The promoters of the business get together, and decide what these statements would be. In doing so, they look at what other companies, especially the seemingly successful ones in that industry, have written. They make a few minor alterations, and there you are. Other companies entering that industry mostly follow suit. At the end of the day, the key players in that industry have strikingly similar vision and mission statements.

In Nigeria's financial services sector, the typical vision statement goes thus:

"To be the leading financial services institution, delivering superior value to all our stakeholders".

It is common to have mission statements that say:

"To provide cutting edge financial solutions to our customers, using a highly skilled and motivated workforce, deploying state of the art technology, while remaining a socially responsible corporate citizen".

While this is not taken from any particular company, it reads like a standard template, which may replace most company's vision and mission without anyone noticing!

Considering what most companies state as their vision and mission, it seems there is limited understanding of the fundamental role of this exercise. There is also a challenge differentiating the specific function of one from the other.

It is generally explained that a company's vision is where it aspires to be, while the mission captures how it intends to get there. This simple explanation can help a lot of companies avoid confusion and the likelihood that their vision and mission statements will remain mere pieces of decoration within company premises. Now let us examine what vision and mission are and what they do for a company.

WHAT IS VISION?

Vision is the imaginative ability to create the picture of a future which is better than the present. Vision requires a rare combination of imagination, intuition and intelligence.

In the world of brands, vision is described as *The reason for being, based on recognized and unrecognized consumer needs or desires. An audacious statement, the vision articulates the brand's aspirations, frames its long term ambitions and essentially captures its point of view of the world.* 1

While our primary aim will be to discuss vision as it relates to building successful brands, it is important to note that most companies do not see vision articulation within the context of branding, but rather as one of the rituals that constitute "pre—operational activities". This assumption explains why a lot of companies have vision statements, while very few actually have a vision. It is also a part of the larger common mistake of perceiving the branding process as a special project rather than an essential part of managing an enterprise.

How is Vision different from Mission and how do they complement each other? Mission is *A statement that describes how the vision can be accomplished, embodying practical business goals. It is ambitious yet achievable over time, and generally reassessed as markets change and the company grows*. 2

Articulating a sound vision requires "great imagination" and prophetic intelligence. This has become even more difficult as technology develops at supersonic speed, rendering certain business models archaic overnight. It helps to think of the vision as a key component of the foundation of a company. It is like the architectural drawing of a building. In 3D, one can see the full picture, even though it does not yet exist. However, it gives a graphic representation of the dream of the founder. This is where great imagination comes in. The ability to visually create what does not yet exist is a critical aspect of what I call "the envisioning" process. Now, imagine that you have seen several building plans and they all look alike. Each new person who desires his own building simply looks at existing architectural drawings and makes a few adjustments. His own plan is ready. In that environment, all the buildings are certain to look alike. Consider also that the builders are likely to buy building materials from the same sources, engage the same laborers and artisans, and you will understand why it is unlikely for any of the house owners to effectively differentiate.

This is similar to what happens in certain industries. Company promoters clone other companies' vision and mission statements, poach each other's key staff, and are constantly watching one another, depending on how keen the competitive pressure is. This explains why company vision and mission statements look alike on the one hand, and on the other hand rarely determine corporate behavior. Most companies already appreciate that differentiation is one of the key objectives of the branding process. What remains is an equal understanding of the fact that the branding process begins with a company's vision. The circumstances leading to the establishment of a company sometimes explain (but never justifies) why due attention is not given to the envisioning process. If a more scientific approach is employed rather than leave this exercise to the discretion of one of the chief promoters of the company, a lot more mileage will be derived.

A well conceived vision consists of two major components – core ideology and an envisioned future. 3.

While the "envisioned future" component is always clearly stated, the "core ideology" part may not always be explicit. In some cases, it is implied in the envisioned future. The Vision Statement of USP Brand Management Consultants, WE SEE A PROSPEROUS AFRICA implies an Afro centric core ideology.

In articulating a sound vision, an important question to ask is "Why do we exist?" It is common to make the mistake of answering this question with "To make profit". This is based on the general belief that every business exists purely for profit. While profit is essential for the survival of the business, it must never be regarded as the company's "reason for being". Companies which focus primarily on profit never last long. This is due to the overriding tendency to see each customer more as an aspect of the company's profit and loss account, than as a person with needs and feelings. When this happens the *raison d'etre* of the business which is to Create Value is undermined. And when a company ceases to create value, it begins to go down.

DEVELOPING A VALUE CREATING VISION

It is important to note that I am not talking of a Vision Statement here, but rather the vision itself. The statement is only a collection of words used to express the vision. In order to ensure that a company's vision is of value to its various stakeholders, let us begin by identifying who these stakeholders are likely to be. Every company exists by virtue of its stakeholders. They fall within four broad categories.

1. Customers
2. Shareholders
3. Employees
4. The Community

In the course of its existence, the company will at different points interact with these stakeholders. Without these groups of people, the company cannot exist. There is therefore a symbiotic relationship, which must be nurtured for as long as the company exists. Each group has its expectations from the company. The success of every company is determined by the extent to which it is able to meet these expectations. It is possible for us to approximate the expectations of each group.

1. Customers expect quality and value for money.
2. Shareholders expect good returns on their investment.
3. Employees expect a conducive and rewarding work environment.
4. The community expects social responsibility.

The creation of value is a pre condition for the survival and ultimate success of a company. You must therefore view your company as an integral part of a larger world, while noting your expected role in that world. At this conceptual stage in every company's life, the temptation to be self centered and egotistical is very strong. This self centeredness often leads to vision statements that focus more on ambition rather than vision. Such statements usually talk of becoming "Number 1", or the "Leader" in the industry. If companies begin with the realization that you cannot become Number 1, on your own, perhaps they will move away from making this their vision statement. While this might make a company's promoters feel good, it could actually limit the company's potential. Within the context of the Vision, becoming an industry leader should be seen as a means to an end, rather than as an end in itself. A value creating vision comes out of a company seeing itself as part of a whole and recognizing its role in making the whole better.

A company's vision must capture the company's understanding of the expectations of all its stakeholders. Beyond the everyday routine of carrying out its operations, the company should realize it has a key role to play in the lives of people. There ought to be a broader understanding of the needs of the community. The vision of a leading player must reflect the sobering appreciation of the responsibilities of leadership, which means that the position must be used for the greatest good of the greatest number of people.

WHAT BRAND VISION DOES

In an ideal situation, the vision should firmly establish a framework for uniting the stakeholders of the company behind a common purpose. This becomes possible when the vision is articulated not merely as a statement but as brand vision.

Articulating a brand vision means taking a brand centric approach to the envisioning process. From the outset, brand vision helps chart a marketing course for the company. When Microsoft envisions a computer in every home and Microsoft in every computer, there is an automatic marketing objective implicitly stated in that vision. Or when a bank envisions its account holder in every home, it instantly sends a compelling message to its stakeholders. Every employee becomes a crusader for the company, taking the bank's offering to all and sundry, and winning converts. This vision will also immediately establish that this is a mass market brand. A niche player cannot reasonably envision its product or service in every home. This will create a conflict between brand vision and brand behavior, a subject extensively treated in Chapter Five.

Brand vision helps you avoid what I call "everybody's vision", which is "to become the leader". Considering that differentiation is fundamental to branding, this should be aimed for, even in the vision of a company. The fact that most companies have similar vision statements is one of the reasons why employees simply regard such statements as of no consequence. However, companies can make their vision statements galvanize employees and make them gravitate towards a common destination. This becomes possible when the vision has a strong influence on the marketing and other activities of the company. This way, even if an employee does not know the company's vision statement by rote, he would still act in alignment with that vision because all key aspects of corporate behavior are determined to move the company towards that vision.

A survey conducted by USP on the Nigerian banking industry, prior to the 2005 consolidation, revealed that 75% of employees within the industry were neither familiar with their bank's vision statement nor could they explain what their bank's vision was. Also guilty in most cases were the front office executives, above whose heads hang the vision and mission statements! Also guilty in most cases, is the front office executive, above whose head hangs the vision and mission statement! The survey sought to measure the gap between corporate vision and employee behavior. While there was similarity in corporate vision as most of the banks aspired for leadership, there was an equal degree of similarity in employee behavior in the sense that it had little bearing on corporate vision.

A company's brand strategy is what often eventually results in leadership. There is an interesting paradox here. If a company pioneers a product or service category, and remains consistent, it enjoys the first mover advantage and invariably becomes the category or industry leader. In such a situation, one could say that the industry or category did not exist, prior to the existence of that company. It is unattractive for anybody to desire leadership of a category or group that does not exist. This is why most category or industry leaders do not have "everybody's vision". It is usually when an industry exists and is already thriving that people develop the ambition to assume its leadership. In this case, the leader now faces the Herculean task of retaining the leadership position, because every entrant into that market or industry is gunning for the leadership position. New entrants now challenge the leader whose marketing strategy forever remains focused on retaining the highly coveted leadership position.

Brand vision draws attention to the effectiveness of aligning business strategy and brand strategy. It helps promoters and employees focus on creating brand value from Day One. If your logo is not going to look like that of your competitor, why should your vision statement read like theirs? Companies should view the Vision Statement as an aspect of brand identity, and indeed it is. If several companies in an industry are aiming for the same destination, they are likely to be doing similar things in order to get there. It then boils down to a matter of who can do the same things faster, better, or cheaper. The competitive pressure increases to unmanageable levels, leading to unethical practices and unprofessional behavior. Companies can build brand equity, more by doing different things than by doing the same things differently.

How do companies attempt to differentiate themselves using their vision and mission statements? Are they focusing more on attaining leadership positions rather than creating value for the customer and other stakeholders?

A look at the vision and mission of several companies reflect a desire for market leadership, without a corresponding desire for value driven differentiation.

For **United Bank for Africa, UBA**, the vision is:

"To be the undisputed leading and dominant financial services institution in Africa."

The mission of the bank is:

To be a role model for African businesses by creating superior value for all our stakeholders, abiding by the utmost professional standards, and by building an enduring institution. 4

For **Intercontinental Bank Plc**, the vision is:

"To be the number one financial institution in Nigeria with a strong global presence."

Mission:

"To help our stakeholders build and preserve wealth."

For these two banks the quest for industry leadership is paramount in their vision statements. While UBA has the African continent as its focus market, Intercontinental Bank is primarily focused on Nigeria, albeit with a vague reference to the global scene, in "a strong global presence". How is this to be determined?

Now let us consider **Zenith Bank**. The vision is:

"To become the leading Nigerian technology-driven, global financial institution, providing distinctly unique range of financial services."

Mission:

"To offer a unique range of financial services that underscore our corporate commitment to customer enthusiasm and value creation for stakeholders."

Again, the quest for leadership is obvious here. However Zenith Bank qualifies the brand of leadership it aspires to achieve, which is "technology-driven". Does the bank aspire to be a global leader of Nigerian origin, or a Nigerian leader that's globally competitive? A better understanding of the competitive structure of the Nigerian banking industry is likely to illuminate the bank's decision to focus its leadership aspirations on the platform of technology and how it can be deployed to enhance service quality. This focus has helped tremendously in creating competitive advantage for the bank.

At the top echelon of the banking industry, where we have the top five, there had been for a long while the question of who is Number One. Prior to the 90s, the top three were unquestionably First Bank, Union Bank and UBA. These were known as The Big Three. To underscore the strength in the size, Union Bank adopted the slogan; big, strong, reliable. However, by the late 90s, some new generation banks were beginning to catch up with those at the top. The fourth position had traditionally been occupied by Afribank. Meanwhile, the industry started using different and sometimes conflicting criteria to determine leadership. This perhaps explains why Zenith Bank in its vision statement attempts to qualify its leadership quest. The bank is thus able to achieve some differentiation in this regard.

For **Bank PHB**, The vision is:

"To be a leading financial institution committed to providing superior Customer service by redefining standards".

Mission:

"To provide innovative solutions to our Customers with passion, while creating optimal value for our stakeholders."

21

Again, we have the quest for leadership in this bank's vision, but the parameters for that quest are not implied. However, the bank talks of "innovative solutions" in its mission which stands as the way it hopes to attain leadership, if we go by the premise that a company's mission is the way it hopes to actualize its vision.

Other companies in this industry with the quest for leadership are:

Fidelity Bank;

Vision: *To be the number one in every market we serve, and for every branded product we offer.*

Mission: *To make financial services Easy and Accessible to our customers.*

First Inland Bank;

Vision: *To be first and distinctive in all aspects of our business.*

Mission: *To delight our customers and other stakeholders through the application of the very best in people, technology.*

Wema Bank;

Vision: *To be one of the top five banks in Nigeria, in terms of total assets, Deposits and profitability.*

Mission: *To be the reference point for value added service, convenience trust and optimize returns to our stakeholders.*

The quest for leadership, which often leads to the articulation of "everybody's vision", is not limited to the banking sector. Let us consider an example from the manufacturing sector. The vision statement of CAP plc is:

"To be the number one in our chosen markets providing exceptional value to our customers." Meanwhile the company's mission is *"To experience the thrill of adding value to the lives and businesses by being a superior convenience provider".*

Why is leadership the first thing a company puts down in black and white, as soon as it is established?

While most players in the banking sector want their places at the top, some dare to be different in articulating their vision and mission statements. And this is not to imply that they do not desire leadership. It is important to focus on altruistic values that have the potential to take companies to the top of their industries, rather than on the desire to be at the top.

Access Bank;

Vision: *"To transform our bank into a world-class financial services provider".*

Mission: *"To go beyond the ordinary; to deliver the perceived impossible, in the quest for excellence".*

This clearly avoids the pitfall of "everybody's vision". But then, the vision sounds more like a special project. With the transformational impact of 21st Century information technology, and the resources available to every Nigerian bank in the post consolidation era, such a transformation should be something like a 24 month project. Given the competitive structure of post consolidation banking, it is virtually impossible for a bank that is not globally competitive to survive for more than a few years.

Diamond Bank;

Vision: *"A strong financial services institution with effective presence in Nigeria and Africa and indeed, in all the key financial centers of the world".*

Mission: *"To create a unique International Bank focused on providing creative solutions to customers' business problems with an absolute commitment to quality."*

While the vision may not be clear and motivational, the bank achieves a significant connection between its mission and its positioning in the industry. Immediately after its recapitalization process, the bank launched a campaign with the promise of helping people bring their business ideas to fruition.

Equitorial Trust Bank;

Brand Vision: *"To be a pace setting institution committed to quality service and staff excellence aimed at achieving customer loyalty and optimum returns."*

Brand Mission: *"To be a highly referenced, efficient, courteous and innovative Bank that combines modern information technology with technical competence to foster an enduring partnership with our customers."*

Significantly, the bank begins by seeing itself as a brand, and immediately establishes the necessary connection between vision and brand strategy. The key phrases "quality service" and "customer loyalty" also reflect the need to articulate a company's vision in a way that it provides a strong platform for the company's marketing strategy. Unfortunately, the vision itself falls short of what a Brand Vision should be. There is hardly anything visionary about being "committed to quality service and staff excellence". The aim of "achieving customer loyalty and optimum returns" equally falls short of being visionary. The aspiration to be a pace setter may be in place but the areas in which the bank aspires to set the pace are generic. The mission is equally replete with clichés. While this may be pardonable in a vision and mission statement, it would be most unexpected from a company that has articulated a Brand Vision and Mission. Within this context, the "brand" idea implies that the company sees the need for differentiation, especially the type that creates competitive advantage.

GETTING YOUR BRAND VISION RIGHT

Companies come into existence for different reasons and under different circumstances. The first question to ask, in the process of articulating a vision statement is; why does this company exist? A lot of entrepreneurs go into business "to make money". While there is nothing wrong with this, a lot is wrong with the belief that every business exists to make profit. Many CEOs have told me "we are a business, and like any other business; we are here to make money for our shareholders".

During a presentation to the management team of one of the banks that survived the financial sector consolidation in Nigeria, a key member of the team was quick to emphasize that the thousands of shareholders who have enabled the bank meet the new minimum capital requirement would only be interested in good returns on their investments. Unfortunately, return on investment is understood only in terms of how much dividends and bonus issues accrue to shareholders at the end of each financial year.

The first thing companies need to understand is that you can not make sustainable profit unless you are able to consistently create value. The process of defining the core purpose of an organization must therefore focus more on creating value, rather than making profit. Creating value in this context refers more to the customers of the company than shareholders. One of the cardinal objectives of the branding process is to create and sustain customer loyalty, since this is the key to the survival of every enterprise.

How do corporate vision and mission contribute, or determine the creation of brand value? Let us begin by analyzing the two most common factors that have beclouded the vision of corporations over the years.

1. The Quest for Leadership

While only very few companies ever create new categories, most companies desire to lead in their respective categories. Meanwhile, experience shows that it is a lot easier to assume leadership of a category, when you create the category. But how many companies are willing to take the high risk of creating a new category? Even though the risk of failure is high, the few companies that are able to successfully pull off the creation of a new category usually emerge leaders in such categories. However, a new category is small and yet unpopular. So the attraction for those hungry for leadership is not strong. But as the category grows, it becomes more attractive. This is when others begin to plot the overthrow of the pioneer/leader of that category. There is therefore a strong tendency for new entrants to focus too much on overtaking the leader while equal attention is not given to creating value. The greater value creator in this situation is the daring company that has created the new category.

There is no category without a leader, even though some category leaders may appear vulnerable to competitive onslaught. Where there is no clear leader, there probably does not yet exist a category. A business plan that seeks to create a new category is always difficult to sell to investors. Yet that is where true vision often lies!

The challenge of retaining leadership is not always well handled by some companies. For this reason, leadership can often be seized by ambitious follower companies. Leadership always means that the leading company becomes the benchmark, against which others in that category measure their success. Taking over the leadership therefore becomes the ultimate aim for most ambitious companies. Since leadership is synonymous with corporate success, it is understandable that most companies will focus on this goal in their vision statements.

2. The Quest for Profit

This is premised on the assumption that all businesses exist for profit. While profit is essential for the survival and success of an enterprise, it should not be the end, or the reason for being. However, the financiers are usually at the fore when a company is being founded. It is therefore understandable that at this stage, managing their expectations assumes paramount importance.

In *"Built to Last"*, Jim Collins and Jerry Porras establish certain characteristics of "truly exceptional and long lasting companies". Drawing upon a six year research project, they clearly identify that profit is usually not seen as the reason for being in companies that achieve superior performance over the long term. It is instructive to note that companies that put altruistic values ahead of the profit motive in their vision statements often appear to be engaged in "idealistic sentiments". Citing the example of the prospectus Masaru Ibuka prepared for the Sony Corporation in 1946, three key definitions of the company's reason for being are highlighted:

1. *To establish a place of work, where engineers can feel the joy of technological innovation, be aware of their mission to society, and work to their heart's content.*
2. *To pursue dynamic activities in technology and production for the reconstruction of Japan and the elevation of the nation's culture.*
3. *To apply advanced technology to the life of the general public.* 5

The company further articulated Management Guidelines, in which it was stated that Sony "shall eliminate any unfair profit-seeking, persistently emphasize substantial and essential work, and not merely pursue growth". Even when forty years later, Akio Morita rephrased the company's ideology, the essential values remained the company's guiding force. Restating the company's commitment to "technological innovation", Morita wrote *Sony is a pioneer and never intends to follow others. Through progress, Sony wants to serve the whole world. It shall be always a seeker of the unknown.* 6

Through the decades, those founding principles have galvanized the Sony workforce to achieving the technological breakthroughs that defined the success of the company. Such innovations include the first all transistor radio in 1955, the first home-use videotape recorder in 1964, the Sony Walkman in 1979, and more recently the phenomenal Sony Playstation. Sony is a perfect example where vision provides a compelling platform for marketing strategy, and other aspects of corporate strategy. The focus was on creating value rather than profit and category leadership. While the quest for leadership and profit did not feature as the company's driving force, Sony became its category leader and sustained superior performance for decades.

John Young, former CEO of Hewlett-Packard was quoted as stating in 1992, that HP had always *remained clear that profit—as important as it is—is not why the Hewlett-Packard Company exists*. 7 Another case study is Merck & Company, whose internal management guide states *We are in the business of preserving and improving human life. All of our actions must be measured by our success in achieving this goal.*.8

How can companies focus their vision articulation on the creation of value, and the establishment of compelling value propositions which will provide the platform for superior performance?

Step One: Make a Value Creation Statement

The first step in articulating a value driven vision statement is to answer the question; why do we exist? In answering this question, you must focus on your customers, rather than yourself. You must avoid what I call "business plan objectives". These are objectives that have to do with the viability of the business, and how much profit the company projects to deliver over a specific number of years. The tendency is for most companies to focus on business plan objectives rather than value creating objectives.

If you are a bank, your vision statement could be:

"To become the number one bank in Nigeria, and indeed the world, in terms of branch network and profitability"

This is typical of everybody's vision and it focuses on business plan objectives, rather than value creating objectives. Yet it sounds more familiar, as it is closer to the vision statements we are likely to more frequently come across. While it captures the ambitions of the promoters of the bank and the envisioned future according to them, it negates the value creating platform, which a brand vision should have. Now let us consider a value driven equivalent of this statement for the same bank:

"To make banking service available to all and affordable by all"

In this statement, the ambition to become number one is not the focus. Rather it is to put service within the reach of everybody. This implies a number of positive messages about the organization.

1. That its service is desirable, and something that everybody deserves.
2. That the service is real value for money since it will be made affordable.

Now if the bank is to make its service available to all, it must go on an aggressive branch expansion policy. This means that the bank must strive to have branches in as many locations as possible. But the emphasis is not on the branches but on the branches' reason for being, which is to provide service. This vision provides a strong platform for developing an effective marketing strategy for the bank, which will have at its heart the dual objectives of availability and affordability.

If the bank is able to constantly live up to this promise, isn't it probable that it will surely move towards becoming number one? While the actualization of this depends on the competitive landscape, competitive activity and how the bank responds to such activity, the vision provides a stronger platform for actionable plans. It projects the institution as a caring company which is not in business solely for profit. If the company aggressively pursues this vision it will grow.

Profit is not something that should be in a company's vision statement. Other companies disguise this in the phrase "deliver superior returns to shareholders" thereby running the risk of losing sight of what matters most—the creation of value for customers.

Step Two: Envision a Better World

Great brands have a way of striking a positive note with humanity. The reasons are clear. There is so much strife and tribulation in the world today that any sincere attempt by any individual or organization to make a positive difference will be most welcome. This is why The Body Shop continues to resonate with humanity on a strong emotive platform. In today's world, an ambitious brand must envision a better world and identify its role in creating that world.

A company, especially one with global ambitions must be able to see its existence and reason for being beyond its immediate environment. It must have a core ideology that transcends national boundaries. This will create a strong foundation for creating value. It will also establish a strong philosophical platform for taking the brand to other countries. In articulating its vision statement, a company must relate its reason for being with the need to make the world a better place.

Step Three: Admit It Is Not Your Company

Successful brands do not belong to their "owners". They belong to the millions of followers who believe in them. This is why the owners of such brands take feedback very seriously. This is why Coca Cola had to rescind its decision to change the coke formula, when the real owners of the brand rejected the new formula. It is important for companies to begin with this reality in mind. A brand is successful only to the extent that it is accepted by people. The tendency is very strong for company promoters to be self centered, focusing on personal ambition and ego, often at the expense of true value creation. This explains why the quest for leadership is prominent in most companies' vision statements.

As "impossible" as it sounds, founders of ambitious companies must develop the discipline to view their companies, not as private possessions, but as an institution held in trust for their millions of prospective customers. While this is not supposed to be explicitly stated in the Vision, it may be implied.

THE SECOND DIMENSION

"

No one buys your product because they want you to make money. Yet you cannot make money unless they buy your product. So what would make them buy your product? You must offer value. In doing this, you must define value not only from your perspective, but from theirs.

"

BRAND VALUE PROPOSITION

For any relationship to stand a chance of survival, or better still, stand the test of time, it has to be built on a symbiotic exchange of value. This exchange derives its meaning from each party's perception of the value being derived. For as long as each party continues to derive value, the relationship will subsist. Value, in this context has to be understood from the perspective of the person concerned. Value is indeed in the eye of the beholder, since what is of value to Mr. A, may be absolutely meaningless to Mr. B.

By the same token, for any brand to command patronage and loyalty, its patrons must be deriving value from their romance with the brand. The branding process is about creating and sustaining that value. And central to that process is the creation and development of a strong and compelling value proposition. This is perhaps the most challenging aspect of branding for most companies. Not only because they often fall short of developing an enduring value proposition, but also because they do not even realize the need for a strong value proposition, as a prerequisite for business success.

The misconception that businesses exist first and foremost to make a profit becomes relevant here. This mindset is one of the obstacles to creating a compelling value proposition. In order to better understand why many companies are unable to offer strong value propositions in their respective markets, let us attempt a better understanding of value and brand value proposition.

WHAT IS A BRAND VALUE PROPOSITION?

What's in it for me?

This is the unspoken question that consumers often ask when making purchase decisions. The question that companies and brand owners need to ask themselves therefore is; how does my brand fare when this question arises? What is in it for whoever is buying my product or service? The fundamental offer of value is a *sine qua non* in creating a brand. A product or service, in its most basic form can be said to exist only when there is some form of value being offered. If a company manufactures detergents, consumers will buy the company's product with the belief that their cleaning needs will be met by using those products. By way of value proposition, the company is saying to prospective consumers; I have a product that can help you solve some of your cleaning problems. This however does not yet qualify as a *brand value proposition*.

Companies will create better value propositions if they think more in terms creating value, rather than making profits. This is because the customer is essentially selfish and will patronize a product or service only because his specific needs are being met by that product or service.

A series of surveys were conducted by USP over the six year period 2001-2007 on patronage drivers in the Nigerian banking sector. Respondents were asked to mention the factors that made them choose the banks they maintained accounts with. Customers of the leading banks responded by mentioning the factors that motivated their patronage. These factors are listed in order of frequency.

FIRST BANK
1. Financial Strength
2. Proximity of Branch
3. Branch Network Size
4. Integrity

UBA
1. Financial Strength
2. Integrity
3. Branch Network Size
4. Proximity of Branch

STANDARD TRUST BANK
1. Branch Network Size
2. Innovative Products
3. Friendly Staff
4. Proximity of Branch

ZENITH BANK
1. Innovation
2. Service Quality
3. Financial Strength
4. Branch Network Size
5. Internet Banking

GUARANTY TRUST BANK
1. Service Quality
2. Recommendation from Friends
3. Proximity of Branch

WEMA BANK
1. Strength and Reliability
2. Proximity of Branch
3. Friendly Staff
4. Integrity

Overall, Proximity is the most frequently mentioned factor as it features for almost all the banks. This is however closely tied to branch network, since the banks with the larger branch networks are also able to achieve better proximity to their customers' homes and businesses. This means that convenience is a major consideration for these customers. Meanwhile, no customer maintained an account with any of these banks because he wanted the bank to make a profit! A close analysis of the reasons given also reveals the essentially selfish nature of the typical customer.

Furthermore, respondents were asked to rank the banks based on the various attributes they considered patronage drivers. The attributes that featured most prominently were

- Innovation
- Dynamism
- Integrity
- Aggressiveness
- Professionalism
- Corporate Social Responsibility

Under each attribute, the banks ranked differently. This is however a reflection of the strengths of each of these banks, from their customers' perspective. In several cases, what a bank touted as its strengths did not feature prominently as a patronage driver for the customers. This disconnect notwithstanding, the customers ranked the banks based on attributes which indicate that value is better defined from the perspective of the customer.

No one buys your product because they want you to make money. Yet you can not make money unless they buy your product. So what would make them buy your product? You must offer value. In doing this, you must define value not only from your perspective, but from theirs.

THERE ARE TWO TYPES OF VALUE

We can speak broadly of two kinds of value in the branding process, namely Tangible and Intangible value. These have also been described as

Economic and Non-economic value, by Professor Das Narayandas of Harvard Business School. 9

Tangible Value

This consists of the functional benefits to be derived from using a product or service. The tangible value to be derived from a car, for example, is transportation. A car takes you from Point A to Point B. This is one of the reasons for purchasing the car. The tangible value to be derived from wearing a shirt is that it covers your body, and protects you from the elements.

Intangible Value

Now, what is responsible for making you buy a particular brand of car? Or as regards clothing, a particular label? Sometimes, this has to do with intangible value, which has been created through the branding process. Intangible value therefore has to do with how a particular brand makes you feel, and not necessarily the function it performs. Ultimately, strong brands are built on intangible value, which is often achieved through a sustained association of the brand with attributes desired by the target consumers. Sustained over time, intangible value invariably translates to tangible value for the brand, by way of higher profit margins and customer loyalty.

CREATING A BRAND VALUE PROPOSITION

When you are seeking employment or a contract with a company, you are most likely to be tasked to demonstrate what you have to offer. They will ask you what your deliverables are. They will ask you what you are bringing to the table. They want to know how your offering is going to create value. If they already have in abundance what you claim to be offering, you are not likely to make progress. The more unique your offering is, the greater your chances. That uniqueness must however be complemented with tangible value. An offering may be unique, yet be of no value to the intended recipient.

Now, how many times do companies put themselves in the interviewee/ contractor position and ask themselves the question; what unique value do we have to offer the customer? With regards to our relationship with our customers and prospective customers, what are we bringing to the table? Is the customer already getting this in abundance from our competitors? Is our offering going to deliver superior value to our customers? Companies must realize that customers and prospective customers are constantly putting them to the same tests that they put contractors and job seekers. This understanding is essential to creating enduring value.

The Three-Way Test

A brand value proposition must pass what I call The Three Way Test.

1. It must be unique
2. It must be desirable
3. It must be deliverable

1. The Test of Uniqueness

Whatever you articulate as your Brand Value Proposition must pass the test of uniqueness. This is critical to the achievement of differentiation, especially in clustered markets. The more intense the competitive environment, the more important the need for uniqueness becomes. This uniqueness must be achieved within the context of creating value, rather than as an end in itself. Oftentimes, companies achieve differentiation without necessarily creating value. When a product or service has passed the test of uniqueness, it is said to possess a Unique Selling Proposition. The USP is what differentiates it from the others, but it does not stop at differentiation. It also provides a compelling selling proposition, which makes it attractive to its target market.

It is not enough to tell me that your product is different. Whatever makes it different must be of value to me. A value driven point of differentiation may be achieved through research. For example, during the process of developing a brand of automotive lubricant for a client, a USP survey revealed that the standard 4 litre packaging of most brands usually caused some spillage during application. The packaging was therefore designed to solve that problem. While a packaging that was remarkably different from that of the competition had been created, the additional consumer value of user friendliness had also been achieved.

2. The Test of Desirability

Perhaps one of the biggest mistakes of 20th Century marketing is the common saying in the marketing communications industry about being able to "sell snow to Eskimos". This is seen as a big complement on a marketer's selling skills, or the effectiveness of advertising creativity. Even if used metaphorically, this idea belongs to those who believe that the test of your marketing communications lies in how convincing you are. This pressure continues to mount on advertising agencies because most companies do not really subject their product concepts to the desirability test. The question to ask is: why sell snow to Eskimos, and not thermal jackets? If indeed you are so convincing he buys the snow from you, is he likely to come back for more? It is a tragedy that this line of thinking still largely drives advertising messages today. This will however be discussed in greater detail in Chapter 6.

The Desirability Test goes well beyond the sort of market research that tells you that if people see the product they would buy. A lot of products have been launched based on this kind of research and they still end up disastrously. However, companies can do a lot better by relying more on consumer insight and an in depth understanding of the dynamics of their immediate market. In developing a product or service, creating consumer value must be the uppermost consideration. A good product is one that when launched, your target consumer instantly feels you have developed the perfect solution to one of his problems. His reaction should be something like: yes, these guys are thinking of me!

3. The Test of Deliverability

One of the attributes of strong and enduring brands is credibility. The more people are able to predict and trust a brand, the stronger the brand tends to be. This trust is however never achieved overnight. It is earned through years of consistency, and of course, sacrifice. This third test is perhaps the most critical, because a promise is only as good as one's ability to fulfill it. Since the Brand Value Proposition is the promise a brand is making, the ability to keep the promise is critical to the success of that brand.

Companies must therefore examine very objectively their ability to deliver consistently on whatever promise they make to their customers. In articulating a value proposition, companies must ask themselves if they have the capabilities to consistently fulfill that proposition. Many companies make the mistake of making promises they cannot keep. This is based on the faulty assumption that the more fantastic your promise is, the more attractive you are to the customer. In truth, the more fantastic the promise, the less credible it is, and the higher the probability that it won't be kept. The average consumer is not necessarily asking for the heavens. The ability to deliver is more important than how fantastic the promise sounds.

Barriers to Creating a Strong Value Proposition

Why do most companies fail at coming up with compelling value propositions?

The Risk Factor

The more unusual an idea seems, the less attractive it is to promoters of new companies, as well as developers of new products. Much of the financing for new companies and products come from banks and non bank financial institutions. And how do they assess the viability of new ventures? They consider whether it is a tested and trusted idea. They consider whether it has worked either in the same environment or in some other environments. If it is an unfamiliar idea, it is perceived as a very risky venture. If it is a familiar idea which has worked, then it is more likely to be considered viable. The downside of this however is that a familiar business or product idea is not likely to pass the **Test of Uniqueness**. The more unique or unusual an idea is, the higher the perceived risk associated with it.

Beware of Consultants!

Every day, conventional management and business consultants are busy cooking up what they understand as value propositions. I have come across numerous such propositions. But I am yet to see one that will pass the Three Way Test. This is why I recommend a distinction between a Value Proposition and a *Brand* Value Proposition. In a similar way, it is possible to draw a distinction between corporate vision and brand vision especially where the company is into manufacturing.

Value proposition, according to conventional management thinking stops at defining what a company is bringing to market. By this thinking, it is normal to have a list of five or more value propositions for a single company or brand, in no particular order. When there is an order to it, it is usually to form an acronym. These propositions are often generic, fuelling the perception among many business executives that "a consultant is one who takes your watch from you and tells you what time it is". Within the context of branding, focus and single-mindedness become paramount in articulating your value proposition.

A Brand Value Proposition goes beyond defining what a company is bringing to market, by subjecting that offering to critical appraisal. This critical appraisal is what I have organized as The Three Way Test. The greatest test to the strength of a market leader's value proposition usually arises when that position is seriously challenged by a competitor. Which brands have strong propositions that pass the Three Way Test? Let us consider a few.

The Celtel Value Proposition

At the 2006 Brand Revolution Conference, where I was one of the speakers, Norman Moyo, the Marketing Manager of Celtel, one of the leading mobile phone networks in Africa did a presentation on the Celtel Brand. The Celtel Brand Value Proposition is *Making Life Better.* He explained how the mobile giant is not about mobile phones but about making a positive impact on the lives of people. Participants were shown how Celtel advertising never shows cell phones, but people from different walks of life.

Does this pass the Test of Uniqueness? In an industry where most players are talking of connection and how their networks help you achieve business success, this is certainly a unique proposition. Does it pass the Test of Desirability? As a dominant network in Africa, where poverty levels are above the global average, the desire for a better life is definitely not far fetched. And is it deliverable? By virtue of the services the company provides, the promise is definitely deliverable. The transformational impact of the telecom networks on the lives of the ordinary people has been tremendous. Meanwhile, the company further supports the promise with promotions, especially the Win Your Dream Promo, in which the star prize is N15million to be spent on any project of the winner's dream.

The Glo Value Proposition

*Glo is the second largest mobile network in Nigeria.*10.

When it was launched in 2003, two years after market leader MTN and Econet Wireless, the network introduced its services with a consumer champion strategy. It became the first network to adopt the per-second billing system. This worked brilliantly, especially at a time there was a general outcry against high mobile phone call rates. Glo's value proposition was based on pocket friendliness and an appeal to national pride. This appeal was also timely, because the nation needed a good dose of patriotic encouragement. Given the ongoing economic and social reforms, Nigerians were indeed in need of national icons. Most of its advertising featured Nigerian celebrities in the entertainment industry, with the pay off line, *glo with pride*. The Glo value proposition was unique, desirable and deliverable. Less than four years later, the company sought to take its brand promise to the next level, and changed its pay off to *rule your world.*

The Bank PHB Value Proposition

Bank PHB resulted from the merger of Platinum Bank and Habib Nigeria Bank. As a result of the banking sector reforms, the total number of banks reduced from 89 to 25 between 2004 and 2006. Consequently, the new competitive landscape required more compelling value propositions and more attractive competitive offering. Bank PHB developed a value proposition hinged on futuristic thinking. "One day cars will run on water," one of its corporate ads proclaims, "At Bank PHB, we are already thinking like that". The bank scores high on the Test of Uniqueness with this futuristic brand promise, and a distinct brand identity. Is this promise desirable? Absolutely! People would definitely like to see a bank that thinks ahead. One of the frustrations of entrepreneurs is that banks are unable to "see" their vision. Therefore, a bank that sees beyond today and is futuristic in its thinking should be a welcome change.

Now, is this promise deliverable? Considering that most breakthrough ideas usually sound stupid initially, is this bank committed to investing in seemingly stupid ideas? Are their criteria for evaluating business plans radically different from that of "conventional" banks? Considering that banking is a highly regulated industry, will they be able to put their futuristic ideas into practice? There is a big question mark here because this futuristic thinking is only to be seen in the bank's advertising. The dangers inherent in making undeliverable promises will be discussed in detail in Chapter 6.

The Emzor Value Proposition

Emzor Pharmaceuticals is Nigeria's leading indigenous pharmaceutical company. The company's value proposition is hinged on the twin promise of affordability and availability. Before Emzor, the pharmaceutical industry was dominated by multinationals. Meanwhile, affordability was never a strong point of these companies. The public healthcare system was way below the expectation of the country's 150 million people. This is coupled with a high poverty level, and a complete absence of health insurance. Within this context, quality drugs that are affordable were definitely a unique and desirable offering. This value proposition is tied to the vision of the company's founder, Stella Okoli. According to her, "the vision has always been to see every Nigerian enjoy quality and affordable healthcare wherever he or she may be in the country". The company became Nigeria's largest indigenous pharmaceutical brand.

However, the uniqueness aspect gradually became undermined with the entry of other indigenous companies who sought to eat into the lucrative analgesic market which had been dominated by Emzor. Prominent among them was Dana Pharmaceuticals which introduced Paradana, its own brand of low priced paracetamol.

The Zenith Bank Value Proposition

Zenith Bank had only recently properly articulated its value proposition, which is hinged on relying on the best people, using state-of-the-art technology to deliver superior service to its customers. The bank has as its pay off; *people, technology, service*. This is compelling and underscores the fact that your technology is only as good as the extent to which it makes life more convenient for your customers. The bank had for years been a leader at deploying advanced technology in banking. The uniqueness of this promise was challenged when on-line real-time banking service became more or less the minimum standard in the industry. The bank however manages to sustain its leadership in the deployment of info tech, especially with the opening of the industry's first ATM Gallery. Other banks are sure to open their own ATM galleries. This means there is some risk in basing your value proposition on non proprietary technology. As long as your competitors have access to that technology, your competitive advantage may not be sustainable.

The IEI Value Proposition

The value proposition of International Energy Insurance, IEI is encapsulated in its *We Care in Three Ways* philosophy. The company cares about its customers' people, businesses and the environment. Coupled with the company's positioning for the energy sector, the promise is unique and desirable. The company delivers on the promise and anchors its social responsibility program on environmental protection.

A compelling and sustainable value proposition is critical to brand success and only brands that are able to achieve this will continue to withstand the offensives that competition will always throw at them.

THE THIRD DIMENSION

"

The fear of a market definition that is "too narrow" is one of the reasons companies fail to develop a strong positioning platform. Yet it is often futile to try being everything to everyone.

"

BRAND POSITIONING

Many businesses are afflicted by a common syndrome. In most cases, it stunts growth and turns the company into a rudderless ship whose course is determined by the waves. I call it the fear of brand positioning. This fear has in fact led to the demise of many an enterprise. According to Philip Kotler,

*Positioning is . . . a powerful tool for creating and maintaining real differentiation in the marketplace.*11.

So why are people afraid of brand positioning? An understanding of the Nigerian business environment as well as the socio economic profile of the population is necessary, in order to get a full understanding of this fear, for it is really not an unfounded fear.

What is Brand Positioning?

Brand Positioning has to do with how you want people to perceive your product or service relative to the competition and the things you do in order to achieve that desired perception. Since Al Ries and Jack Trout developed the concept of Brand Positioning, marketing has witnessed a fundamental shift from the days of the Four Ps. Companies now realize more than ever before the importance of managing perception as a key part of the marketing function.

Positioning starts with a product. A piece of merchandise, a service, an institution, or even a person.12. Brand Positioning is the way you apply the concept of positioning in your branding process, towards determining the space you want to occupy in the prospect's mind.

> *But positioning is not what you do to a product. Positioning is what you do to the mind of the prospect.*
> *So it's incorrect to call the concept "product positioning." You are not really doing something to the product itself.*
> *Not that positioning doesn't involve change. It often does. But changes made in the name, the price, and the package, are really not changes in the product at all. They are basically cosmetic changes done for the purpose of securing a worthwhile position in the prospect's mind*. 13

While this may be true of positioning, there is a danger in the submission that positioning is not what is done to the product but to the mind of the prospect. The danger here is that the view supports the notion that branding is by and large a cosmetic exercise.

> *To equate "brand" with such superficial cosmetics is the equivalent of saying that people are only really the sum of their name, face and clothes*. 14.

The Business Environment in Nigeria

The business environment evolved from the oil boom in the 70s, austerity measures in the 80s, economic depression in the 90s and economic reforms in the early years of the 21st Century. Signs of a slowdown first emerged about the end of the 70s. But official acknowledgement only followed during the Second Republic Government of Shehu Shagari(1979-1983) with the introduction of what was then referred to as Austerity Measures. This comprised a series of measures aimed at achieving the twin objectives of enforcing fiscal discipline in the administrative apparatus of government and diversifying the economy. Unfortunately, the government was unable to see that programme through.

By the late 80s, the Military Government introduced the Structural Adjustment Programme, SAP, with the objective of creating a liberalized private sector led economy. Against this background were rising unemployment rates and rising inflation in a market dominated by imported goods. Between 1985 and 1995, the economy witnessed what has been described as the disappearance of the middle class. The market was characterized by a social structure which consisted of the haves and the have nots, with an ever widening gap in between. In this situation only two categories of goods could thrive. Those designed for the upper class and those for the masses.

With the coming of another democratic government in 1999, a new economic reform programme was unveiled. A key aspect of the new economic reforms was the liberalization of the telecoms sector. An erstwhile monopoly by government owned NITEL gave way to the emergence of Private Telecom Operators, PTOs. With such rapidly changing economic policies, businesses have had to rapidly adapt to often unpredictable developments.

It is a paradox that while brand strategy holds the key to overcoming most business challenges, those business challenges actually prevent people from developing brand strategy.

I was discussing with the newly appointed CEO of an ailing bank sometime in 2005. When I told him of the need to develop a sound brand strategy for the bank, he replied that what they needed at the bank was not a brand strategy but a survival strategy. In my own world, there is no better survival strategy than a good brand strategy. But then, it is all a function of what the gentleman understands as brand strategy. Considering that branding was largely perceived as a cosmetic exercise it is no surprise that some people would draw such a definite line between brand strategy and survival strategy. Yet this is not peculiar to Nigeria.

This less than adequate understanding of the nature and role of brands and branding is illustrated with an example cited in The Economist's

Brands and Branding, published in 2003. In response to an approach from a brand consultancy, the CEO of a FTSE company wrote **Branding is not our preoccupation at the moment**. 15. In the face of difficult market conditions, top management is often preoccupied with "more important things", such as cutting costs and restructuring.

TYPES OF POSITIONING

Positioning may be approached either by market segment or by product features.

Positioning By Market Segment

A brand may be positioned according to the market segment it is designed to serve. The most common indicator of this kind of positioning is price. A low priced product is considered positioned for the masses at the bottom of the pyramid, while high priced products are presumed to be meant for the elites at the top.

Positioning By Product Features

Companies also use product features to achieve their desired positioning in the market. For example, working with one of the independent petroleum marketing companies to develop a new brand of automotive lubricants, we had sought to position the brand as "user friendly", by designing a packaging that eliminated the spillage associated with most other brands.

Common Dilemmas in Brand Positioning

What happens to a brand when it is caught in a situation of pessimism about future revenue from its niche positioning? Should the brand shift its customer base and reposition?
What happens to a mass market brand when the high profit margin of the premium market becomes too attractive to resist?

These are common dilemmas that brand custodians often face when there is a belief that an opportunity exists outside a brand's core market segment.

WHAT IS A MASS MARKET BRAND?

When a brand is differentiated by market segment, it becomes either a mass market or a luxury brand.

A mass market brand is the brand that appeals to the lower and larger segment of the market. Affordability and availability are usually key factors that drive the patronage and loyalty of a mass market brand.

Market structures differ from country to country. This means a mass market brand in one country may be a premium or luxury brand in another market. This is determined by average living standards.

EXAMPLES OF MASS MARKET BRANDS

Cowbell Milk

The economic depression of the 80s put dairy products beyond the reach of the masses in Nigeria. Promasidor identified an opportunity and introduced the Cowbell brand in easily affordable packaging. With a price tag of just N5.00 per sachet and nationwide distribution, it was a true mass market brand.

Indomie Noodles

The leader in the noodles category is Indomie Noodles which is effectively distributed across the country, and affordably priced.

Emzor Paracetamol

Emzor Pharmaceuticals identified a need, and decided to produce quality products that are readily available and affordable. Emzor Paracetamol is the flagship brand from the company, based on that strategy.

Coca-Cola

The number one soft drink brand globally, and a mass market brand in all the markets in which it is available.

The brand successfully reaches the mainstream markets wherever it is sold.

WHAT IS A LUXURY BRAND?

A luxury brand, on the contrary is designed essentially for the discerning and elitist consumer. They are mainly prestige brands. Social gratification and approval are primary factors that drive the patronage of luxury brands.

Luxury brands often identify niche markets and seek to occupy such niches. Expectedly, luxury brands are priced beyond the reach of the masses.

EXAMPLES OF LUXURY BRANDS

Lexus

This is an automobile brand from global automaker, Toyota. Lexus brand was created to allow Toyota play in the luxury segment.

Rolex

For decades, the Rolex brand has remained the definitive standard in luxury wrist watches. It is today the world's leading luxury brand of wrist watch.

Mont Blanc

This is the world's number 1 brand of writing instruments. Note that Mont Blanc describes their brand as "writing instruments", as a way of elevating them above the more familiar "pen".

SOME BRANDS CUT ACROSS

Honda manufactures a wide range of equipment and automobile.
In the auto segment, Honda brands reach between lower middle to upper middle segments.

Yamaha

The Yamaha brand is over 100 years old. The company manufactures a wide range of machinery and equipment. There are 10,000 naira portable generators as well as 2,000,000 naira acoustic pianos.

Nokia

This is the world's leading mobile handset brand. The company makes handsets for both mass and luxury segments of the markets. There are also a lot of models in between.

LG

After re-branding the LuckyGoldstar brand as LG, the brand rapidly grew into one of the world's leading names in electronics and home appliances. LG products cut across different market segments with a wide range of products.

What Is The Dilemma?

To understand why there may be a dilemma for a lot of companies regarding which segments to play in, it is important to examine the pros and cons of each of the key segments.

ADVANTAGES OF MASS MARKET POSITIONING

1. Lower production costs based on volume.
2. High brand awareness and visibility.
3. High sales volume.
4. Lower per unit marketing cost.

5. High market share.

DISADVANTAGES

1. High distribution costs.
2. Pressure to maintain competitive price.
3. Faking and imitation is easy.
4. Slim profit margins.

ADVANTAGES OF LUXURY BRANDS

1. Command premium price and high profit margins.
2. Exclusivity creates brand equity.
3. Lower distribution costs.
4. Higher brand loyalty.

DISADVANTAGES

1. Small market share.
2. Limitations on growth and expansion due to need to protect brand essence.
3. Attractive to imitators.

CREATING A BALANCE

The question is; is there a need to create a balance? Should luxury brands attempt to stretch to other market segments, and should mass market brands attempt to stretch into the luxury segments? We shall illustrate this dilemma with a few Nigerian brands.

GTBank

This is an example of a luxury brand that is now faced with the challenge of reaching into other market segments

The Story of GTBank

When Guaranty Trust Bank was established in 1989, the vision was to create an elitist financial institution that would set new standards in customer service. The minimum amount to open an account at GTB was well above the industry standard, and the bank employed a screening system for prospective account holders. The essence was to create snob appeal.

The bank deliberately avoided opening too many branches. Initial branches were located in Lagos, Abuja and Port Harcourt. That strategy accounts for why GTBank is today trying to play catch up in terms of branch network. By the time the bank went public in the mid 90s, the story changed. As a public limited and publicly quoted company, the bank had to begin driving growth aggressively. New branches had to be opened.

New market opportunities had to be identified. In other to capture small business enterprises, the bank created advantium, a small enterprise banking package. That initiative flopped, as it remained elitist in terms of delivery. The perception that the bank has no time for small business persisted.

GTBank's Dilemma

The service platform on which the bank differentiated itself is no longer sustainable, as other banks have caught up. The bank needs to continue growing, especially with the newly increased share capital. In spite of the growth, the bank needs to protect its brand essence. The Bank has handled this challenge with remarkable success. While expanding the branch network, the bank has jealously protected its elitist brand status. One brilliant way it has done this is by making an architectural statement with every branch it opens. The bank has demonstrated very clearly that you can retain your premium brand essence, while stretching into new market segments.

THE STORY OF GLO

Coming after Econet and MTN who were already enjoying a head start in the GSM segment, Glo needed an aggressive market entry strategy. The network smartly latched on to the per second billing method, creating the perception of customer friendliness and affordability. This approach immediately endeared the network to the masses of price sensitive subscribers. MTN held on tightly to the upper segment, while Econet was somewhat in between. Glo captured the lower segment of the market. Having dominated the lower segments, Glo needed to enter the more lucrative upper segment. While it enjoyed a wide subscriber base, MTN remained the most profitable network, as it had on its network those who could afford to spend more time talking. In order to enter this segment, Glo created Glo Premium, and launched a campaign using celebrity endorsement. The approach fell short of expectations, as with most celebrity endorsement campaigns. The so called big boys are simply reluctant to be on the same network with their driver. Glo eventually succeeded in penetrating the premium segment of the market by being first to launch the Blackberry Service in Nigeria.

THE FEAR OF STRATEGIC POSITIONING

Sometime in 2004, our company USP was invited by CELLCOM, one of the private fixed wireless telecom operators to come up with a campaign strategy for it. After a couple of briefing sessions with the management of the company, we came up with a positioning platform for the company. The strategy was to position CELLCOM as "the business network". This was based on the premise that there was no telecom network so positioned. The most lucrative users of telecom services in the country were business users. A strong network is the backbone of business, be it a telecom network or a social network. The management of CELLCOM rejected the proposal. Their argument was that the positioning was "too narrow" and they stood the risk of losing out on other segments of the market.

The network eventually engaged one of the leading advertising agencies in the country and launched a campaign touting "freedom" as its campaign theme. Less than three years later the market was virtually "free" of CELLCOM.

The fear of a market definition that is "too narrow" is one of the reasons companies fail to develop a strong positioning platform. Yet it is often futile to try being everything to everyone.

In February 2005, we made a presentation to Bellview, an airline which had operated successfully for about 13 years and was enjoying a dominant position in the industry. It had become the airline preferred by business travelers due to its reliability and promptness. Top company CEOs and government officials were the airline's regular customers.

But stiff competition had now landed with Virgin Atlantic operating in Nigeria as Virgin Nigeria. The very busy Lagos-Abuja route which Bellview had dominated with its Shuttle Service was definitely going to be threatened. It was obvious that the airline would need to respond very quickly and strengthen its hold on the business travelers. We presented a positioning strategy to the management of Bellview, with a view to achieving this objective as well as developing a strong value proposition which would make the airline the first choice for business travelers. In view of the size of Virgin which the small Bellview could not challenge, it became obvious (or so we thought) that a niche positioning was the key to survival.

Unfortunately, the airline refused to toe that line, choosing rather to continue with its campaign slogan of "the preferred airline". It equally turned down proposals for a better organized visual identity. Less than two years later, it struggled as Virgin had completely taken over the lucrative Lagos-Abuja route, operating eight daily flights, compared with Bellview's three. The elite business travelers who had hitherto been loyal to Bellview had almost completely migrated to Virgin. Bellview had failed to use positioning to differentiate itself and retain its core customers. A few years later, Bellview was finally grounded.

BRAND POSITIONING AND PERCEPTUAL MAPPING

Perceptual Mapping is the technique used to visually represent how consumers perceive competing products and services and consumers' preferences for these products and services. It has been used as a strategic management tool for more than thirty years and offers a unique ability to communicate the complex relationships between marketplace competitors and the criteria used by buyers to make purchase decisions and recommendations. 16.

Perceptual Mapping can be used to plot the interrelationships between consumer products, industrial goods, institutions and people. Any product or service that can be rated on a range of attributes can be mapped to show their positions in relation to the competition as well as to the evaluative attributes. Perceptual Mapping is useful in market segmentation, concept development and especially in the development of positioning strategies.

THE FOURTH
DIMENSION

"

Oftentimes there is a gap between the identity a company aims to create and what it actually ends up with. Several factors may be responsible for this. While the process of creating the visual identity is critical, subsequent communication and brand behavior also play a role in shaping people's perception of a company's identity.

"

BRAND IDENTITY

The most easily recognizable aspect of brand identity is the visual aspect. This is what people see and remember. Yet there is more to brand identity than meets the eye. What constitutes the identity of a brand is a combination of many things. Identity must be able to appeal not only to the sense of sight but the other senses as well.

*It must be visible, tangible and all embracing.*17

Every organization is unique and the identity must spring from the organization's own roots, its personality, its strengths and its weaknesses . . . .

Everything that the organization does must be an affirmation of its identity. The buildings in which it makes things and trades, its offices, factories and showpieces-their location, how they are furnished and maintained-are all manifestations of identity. 18

Oftentimes, there is some confusion regarding the distinction between Brand Identity and Visual Identity. While the former embraces the entire identity elements of a brand, including characteristics and personality, the latter is limited only to visual elements. This confusion arises mainly because the visual aspect is what often makes the deepest impression on people. This has given rise to the tendency for companies to focus 80% of their efforts on visual identity, while other identity elements receive a mere 20% attention. The reverse should indeed be the case.

The aim of every company should be to create a unique and enduring brand identity. This begins with brand definition, which is the process of articulating the company's *raison d'etre*.

THE THREE DIMENSIONS OF IDENTITY

There are three key dimensions to brand identity. These are;

1. Essential Identity
2. Desired Identity
3. Perceived Identity

ESSENTIAL IDENTITY

This is the essence of a product or organization. Skye Bank is essentially a bank, just as Carat Medicated Soap is essentially a brand of medicated soap. The essential identity of a product or organization is often closely tied to its functional benefits. However, some companies go the extra length of articulating their Brand Essence, which communicates a creation of value beyond the functional benefits that they have to offer.

DESIRED IDENTITY

The kind of image a company desires to create in the minds of its various target publics has been described in different ways. Terms like Desired Image and Desired Perception have been used. However, what is clear is that companies now realize that they can no longer leave their image to chance, but must rather develop a deliberate strategy for articulating what their objectives are and what they must do to achieve those objectives.

The days are gone when a company CEO would simply ask his grade 4 artistically talented son to design a logo for his company. Now the best qualified professionals are engaged to develop visual identity. Several years ago, you could hardly talk of a company's desired identity. Most companies just wanted to get on with business and make money. Not anymore. With ever increasing competition, companies now realize that planning and deliberately designing an identity has a key role to play in brand success!

Desired Identity is therefore the picture you want people to see of you and the feeling you want them to have about you. Creating that desired picture is then a function of the visual identity elements; colors, logo, and other visual communications. On the other hand appealing to the other senses has to do with brand promise and delivery.

PERCEIVED IDENTITY

This may be described as an aggregation of the identity of a brand as seen by a cross section of the brand's target publics.

Oftentimes there is a gap between the identity a company aims to create and what it actually ends up with. Several factors may be responsible for this. While the process of creating the visual identity is critical, subsequent communication and brand behavior also play a role in shaping people's perception of a company's identity.

In multi-cultural societies like Nigeria, it is critical to approach the brand identity task with great caution. Since origin is central to creating a unique brand identity, the challenge here is to retain an element of your brand's origin without losing universal appeal.

VISUAL IDENTITY

This refers to the symbols, colors, images and devices used to identify a brand and differentiate it from others. Visual Identity has perhaps received more than its fair share of attention in the branding process. This is understandable. More than 90% of the time, our judgment is shaped by appearance. Even though we are often reminded not to judge a book by its cover and that "appearances can be deceptive", we are still overwhelmingly inclined to draw quick conclusions from appearances. This is why brand owners believe in the power of visual impact.

CREATING A POWERFUL LOGO

The logo is the central and most important element of visual identity, especially with corporate brands. In numerous instances it will be the first contact most people have with the company.

A logo is a distinguishing mark for a company, a product, a service or a range of products or services from the same source . . . . A logo is unique to the company it represents, and can be protected legally as a trade mark, trade name or registered mark . . . . A logo can be typographical, figurative, abstract or can be a combination of these . . . . A logo is one of the base elements in a corporate identity or brand identity . . . . A logo can be two or three dimensional, monochrome or colored (though there is normally a two dimensional version for a 3D logo and a black and white version for a colored one).19

A logo is the heart and soul of any visual identity. In simple terms, your logo should reflect who you are (essential identity), where you are coming from (origin) and where you are going (aspirations). Yet all of these must be achieved without letting go of simplicity. The process of logo creation should therefore not be oversimplified as many business owners are wont to do.

WHAT A LOGO IS AND WHAT IT'S NOT

According to Jared McCarthy,

Your logo is not your brand. Your logo only represents your brand. If you're thinking that changing or creating a logo is the same thing as changing or creating a brand, someone's been feeding you some very bad information. Branding and logos are totally separate discussions.

And while your logo is not your brand, it will affect how your brand will be perceived. A great logo can give you incredible leverage and contribute directly to your bottom line.20

Because the logo is often the single most visible and consistently applied element in the overall visual identity, people tend to equate it with brand identity. While the logo is one aspect of visual identity, visual identity is in turn one aspect of brand identity. The logo is probably the singular most important symbol of the promise your brand makes to people.

Some key considerations must be in focus when developing a new logo. These include:

* Simplicity, uniqueness and easy recognition.
* Easy and consistent reproduction across different platforms or surfaces.
* Communication of the Brand Essence.
* Elegance and conformity with the professional standards of design.
* Audience appeal, with particular reference to target publics.

WHEN IS A NEW LOGO NECESSARY?

If you are considering a change or replacement of your existing logo, stop right now.
Changing or replacing your existing logo is tantamount to divorce. The ramifications can wreak havoc on your marketing, your brand, your advertising, customer loyalty, and ultimately, short and long-term sales.

Cleaning, polishing and streamlining your existing logo may be all you really need. If your heart is set on a change, think seriously about updating your logo with a tweak or two while maintaining the overall shape and base design. It's a much safer option than abandoning an icon that is familiar to your existing customer base. 21

PRUDENT BANK PLC

In late 2001, USP started a quiet revolution in corporate branding in Nigeria when the company was engaged to create a new logo for Prudent Bank during the bank's repositioning and restructuring exercise.

Prudent Bank had hitherto been a small and conservative merchant bank. When the regulatory authorities began to allow merchant banks to convert to retail banking, a group of investors bought into the bank and began the process of converting it to a commercial retail bank. This process necessitated a complete branding and repositioning program.

USP's role included visual identity design, positioning strategy and brand communications. Even though it was a small family owned bank, the bank was proud of its past and wanted that heritage reflected in the new identity. The result is a positioning platform anchored on relationships. This includes the relationship between the past and the present as well as the relationship between the bank and its customers. To capture this in a simple yet striking way, the logo has an interlocking symbol which represents these relationships. The bank's positioning statement is *THE SYMBOL OF RELATIONSHIP.*

This platform was to drive the bank's customer service and deliberate efforts were made to cultivate and build mutually rewarding relationships with customers.

*   *Prudent Bank's logo had the 'symbol' of relationship as its most unique element*

For the first time in the country, the bank ran a series of ads that actually explained its visual identity elements. This ad was also framed and placed in every branch of the bank so that staff would imbibe the core message and make it a way of life.

To underscore the emphasis on relationships, the bank designed its branches in such a way that the traditional service counter was tucked further into the banking hall, as far away from the main entrance as possible. The effect was that when you entered a Prudent Bank branch, you would be met by people, not a "barrier". The bank went ahead and put service practices in place to support this positioning statement. Three years later, an independent survey by Marketing & Management Magazine, M2, rated the bank "Most Friendly". This was one of the most successful identity programs in Nigeria's corporate history.

BANK OF INDUSTRY

The task that faced the management of Bank of Industry in 2001 was to build a strong brand from the merger of three financial institutions with separate mandates. The bank emerged from the merger of Nigerian Industrial Development Bank, NIDB; Nigerian Bank for Commerce and Industry, NBCI and National Economic Reconstruction Fund, NERFUND.

USP developed a new Corporate Identity that represents the history and promise of the bank. This is symbolized by the three wheels of progress. The brand strategy was developed on the positive platform of value and revolved around the core attributes of Enterprise, Excellence and Empowerment, known as the 3 Es of BOI.

*   *The 3 wheels of progress in the Bank of Industry logo symbolize Enterprise, Excellence and Empowerment*

UNITY BANK PLC

The largest and perhaps most challenging merger in the banking history of Nigeria is that of the nine banks that made up UNITY BANK PLC. The task of creating a compelling value proposition that would not only unite the various entities but also appeal to the bank's customers and other stakeholders was given to USP. The process led to the creation of what was called the Hexalix, the six sided symbol which showed the bank's national character and presence in the country's six geo political zones.

There are many images that can be seen in the Hexalix. There are human heads surrounding a star. The star stands for the customer, to demonstrate that the customer is at the centre of the bank's world. A white star is formed around the grey star. This white seems to be in motion. The Hexalix is such a powerful and unique symbol it reveals more of itself as you keep looking. More importantly, it illustrates the bank's promise of *SUCCEEDING TOGETHER*.

*   *Unity Bank's Hexalix had the star which represents the customer at the centre*

CRYSTALIFE ASSURANCE

When it became necessary for Equity Indemnity Life Insurance to change its name, a new identity became mandatory. Against the background of insurance companies trying, often unsuccessfully, to sell insurance rather than a strong value proposition, a brand promise of THE BETTER LIFE was created for the company. The company was positioned as protecting and enriching lives. This promise is captured in the logo.

CRYSTALIFE

The Better Life

*   *The Crystalife Assurance logo captures the promise of a better life for the family*

FIRST BANK PLC

First Bank Plc is the oldest bank in Nigeria. It was established as Nigeria's branch of Barclays Bank in 1894. For decades, the bank dominated the sector, and remained the undisputed leading bank in the country until the consolidation exercise in the sector which started around 2003 and led to a series of mergers and acquisitions. The bank had been proactive and dynamic in retaining its leadership position in what had been a rapidly changing financial landscape. It was therefore hardly surprising when in 2004 it embarked on a logo change and identity program. It turned out to be one of the most successful identity programs in the banking sector.

Prior to the change, the central element in the First Bank logo was the elephant, which symbolized financial strength, stability and authority. The bank wisely decided to retain the elephant. The bank's designers might have taken some load off the elephant's back and given it movement, but the elephant survived that exercise, which is why that identity program was a success story. The First Bank story is an excellent example of doing only what is necessary and getting it right.

*   *Old logo of First Bank of Nigeria Plc*

*   *New logo gives 'movement' to the bank's iconic elephant*

GTBANK PLC

Guaranty Trust Bank was established in 1989, and is one of the "new generation" banks. The bank promptly set new customer service standards hitherto unknown in the banking industry. It ran an advertising campaign in the early 90s that people remembered two decades later. It pioneered a number of innovations in customer service that later became industry standard. As the wave of consolidation and brand re engineering overtook the industry, Guaranty Trust embarked on its own identity program. In its own case, it opted for an entirely new logo. When the new logo was unveiled, Guaranty Trust Bank became known as GTBank. The original name logo was changed to the orange square.

■ GUARANTY TRUST ■

*   *Original logo of Guaranty Trust Bank Plc*

*   *The bank's new logo highlights the orange colour to underscore 'passion'.*

The campaign that announced the logo change was a clear indication of the bank's dilemma. The central message in the campaign was that the logo was the only thing that changed about the bank. Every other thing was as it was. To understand this dilemma, one needs to understand how strong the brand was, within the banking sector. Within 15 years, the Guaranty Trust brand had come to symbolize everything a typical Nigerian Bank wanted to be. It was consistently rated high in terms of customer service. Its stock was one of the best performing on the Nigerian Stock Exchange. The bank was professionally run, and had built a solid reputation anchored on the highest professional standards of ethics and integrity. The bank realized the need for extreme care in safeguarding the brand equity it had taken so much time and resources to build. The campaign tried, too hard perhaps, to re assure the bank's stakeholders that nothing except the logo had changed. That campaign was followed up with the Orange Rules campaign, which sought to portray the bank as more "orange" than the Orange Telecoms the whole world knows.

If nothing had changed about the bank, the question is; why change the logo? If the brand had not changed, what is the justification for changing the symbol that represents it? The most essential value proposition people expect from their bank is stability and security, not change. It is the peace of mind that comes from knowing there won't be unpleasant surprises. Unlike fashion, when it comes to where people keep their life savings, they want things to remain as they are, as much as possible.

Was it necessary to change the logo? Has the change done more harm than good? Says Jared McCarthy:

"Agencies and creative types are always prepared to give you a million good reasons that you should make the change. From their side of the table, an overhaul of your corporate ID package is very big, very easy money . . . . But the reality is that unless your current logo is hurting you in a measurable way . . . you should leave it alone".

ZENITH BANK

As the wave of logo change and identity programs swept across the financial services sector, some banks resisted the logo changing fad, and wisely stuck to what had worked for them over the years. One of them is Zenith Bank. Long before other banks woke up to the style, Zenith Bank had been building a strong corporate identity by creating identical branches. You could tell a Zenith Bank branch, even before you saw the name. The bank had long realized that the logo is only one aspect of identity. Of course, Zenith Bank continues to maintain its leadership position in the industry.

ZENITH BANK LIMITED

*   *Zenith Bank has remained consistent with its 'Z' symbol.*

SOMETIMES A NEW LOGO IS A MUST!

If a logo is a symbolic representation of a brand, it stands to reason that the logo should project the essence of that brand. Sometimes a company may be going through changes so fundamental that a new identity becomes a necessity. Mergers are a typical example. As was witnessed during the consolidation of the banking sector, most of the banks that emerged out of mergers needed to create new identities. In some cases, this led to what I call *brandicide*-the painful termination of otherwise strong and promising brands.

SKYE BANK PLC

One of the post consolidation banks is SKYE BANK, the result of the merger of six banks, namely Prudent Bank, Eko International Bank, Bond Bank, Reliance Bank and Co-Operative Bank. The strongest of the five banks without doubt was Prudent Bank. Bond Bank was promising, but was at that time barely three years old. Eko International Bank was state owned and quite strong. The greatest challenge in situations like this is being able to create a strong enough platform to launch the new entity.

Skye Bank got its name from the value proposition of limitless possibilities and opportunities that the sky suggests. Implied is also the general motivational saying of reaching for the sky or the sky being one's limit. Then the bank presented its brand promise as *EXPANDING YOUR WORLD*.

Speaking on the challenges before the brand, its CEO, Akinsola Akinfemiwa said, "In a crowded market we had to be different. We wanted to come up as a bank that cares. We realized that people love to hate banks, so we wanted to show that this bank has time for you. We wanted to create a brand that people will not hate. We wanted an easily recognizable name, universally appealing and fun".

*   *The Skye Bank logo projects simplicity and fun.*

INTERCONTINENTAL BANK PLC

Intercontinental Bank commenced operations in 1989, as Nigerian Intercontinental Merchant Bank Limited, NIMBL. Just like Prudent Bank, it was originally a merchant bank, only much bigger. When the bank eventually exchanged its merchant banking license for a commercial banking one, it simply dropped "Merchant" from its name, making it "Nigerian Intercontinental Bank Limited". When it went public, it became Intercontinental Bank Plc. On both occasions the slight modification had applied only to the name.

During the consolidation era, the bank acquired three other banks with which it had common ownership. The next question was; what do we do about our logo? The bank's management was rightly of the opinion that what the bank needed was the First Bank treatment. USP Brand Management was given the brief. This led to the development of a more visible visual identity, which retained the essential elements of the bank's original logo.

Somehow, the bank later decided that it needed an even newer and more visible visual identity. What resulted was not merely a slight modification but a drastic change.

* *The original logo of Intercontinental Bank portrays the bank's essential conservatism.*

* *The logo was modified to achieve greater brand visibility, without losing the iconic hexagon.*

Intercontinental

BANK

* *Less than two years later, a drastic departure from tradition!*

Oftentimes it is difficult to tell if a logo change has done more harm than good, but a couple of years after the change, the banking sector was hit by financial crises. The sometimes unhealthy rivalry that existed amongst the banks intensified, and Intercontinental Bank claimed some banks were "demarketing" it, *demarketing* being a new coinage to describe a practice whereby other banks spread misleading information about the bank's financial health. Could this logo change have contributed to the negative impact that *demarketing* had on Intercontinental Bank?

Age has always been source of strength or weakness because longevity is an indication of stability and security. Sometimes a radical logo change creates the impression of newness and youthfulness, and by implication could suggest that the company is young. Is the attribute of youth a strength in banking? As a bank gets older, its identity (logo inclusive) becomes an asset of ever increasing value and must be guarded most jealously!

SENSUAL IDENTITY

In developing brand identity, some brands go the extra mile of creating unique identity elements that appeal to other senses, apart from the sense of sight. Generally, perfume brands try to appeal to the sense of touch (the bottles come in unusual shapes) and sense of smell. A lot of brands also create unique sounds with which people identify them. Perhaps the most popular is the Nokia ringtone. Once you hear it, you know it's a Nokia ringing, whether you see the phone or not. The Sony Trinitron makes a unique sound when it is switched on. The extremely popular Motorola Razr phone appeals to the sense of touch. You just like to feel it in the palm of your hand! Most cell phones are now designed to appeal to this sense. The unique shape of the Coca Cola bottle appeals to the sense of touch.

NAMING AND IDENTITY

There is a school of thought that asks "What's in a name?" According to this school, your name might well be anything. What really matters at the end of the day is what the name stands for in the minds of people. While this is to a large extent true, some companies have leveraged the importance of an appropriate name to build strong brands. In several cases also, choosing the wrong name has the potential to do incalculable damage to brand equity.

During the mid to late 90s, the Nigerian banking sector witnessed several takeovers as a result of distress in the industry. Some weak banks were taken over by new investors and in some cases their names were changed. What happened to some of the banks is a study in how NOT to name a company. As is the case with logos, it is often better not to change a company's name. Let us look at a couple of examples.

GAMJI BANK was taken over by new investors, and was renamed International Trust Bank. Now GAMJI is the name of a tree found in the Savannah region of the country. The tree has a very large trunk, is very resilient and grows to a massive size in spite of harsh weather conditions. Isn't it obvious that this is a most appropriate name for a bank? What it tells us is that this bank is strong and can withstand the challenges of a rapidly changing economy. Bank customers constantly need that kind of reassurance especially in a developing economy. The bank might not have lived up to its name, but the new owners did worse. International Trust Bank is completely meaningless, compared to where the bank was coming from. The bank was eventually acquired.

Then there was OWENA BANK, which took its name from a popular river in the Southwest region of the country. The bank was renamed OMEGA BANK. The hidden resources of the ever flowing river could provide a strong analogy for the positive brand characteristics of a bank. I do not know the end of what OMEGA signifies!

When CRYSTAL BANK was acquired, its name was changed to STANDARD TRUST BANK. The enviable qualities of the crystal must have informed the choice of that name by the founders of the bank. But what strong attribute does Standard Trust connote?

When MERCHANT BANK OF COMMERCE was changing to commercial banking, it was renamed CONTINENTAL TRUST BANK. While the former name is descriptive, and instantly communicates the strategic focus of the bank, the latter communicates nothing unique about the bank.

At that time, it seemed every bank wanted to put "trust" in its name, as if that was enough to win customers' trust. With those changes, the industry lost the opportunity to build a globally competitive brand whose name would give a clear indication of its origin.

Many companies take naming seriously enough to engage professionals in the process. When Intercontinental Bank Plc was developing its savings product for younger savers, the bank engaged USP Brand Management, with a brief that included the naming of the product. The result was HAPPY SAVERS, a name developed to align with and reinforce the bank's value proposition of HAPPY CUSTOMER, HAPPY BANK.

The life insurance company formerly known as EQUITY INDEMNITY INSURANCE engaged USP in the process of changing its name to CRYSTALIFE ASSURANCE, and creating a new identity.

CREATING A STRONG IDENTITY

Creating a strong identity begins with articulating a Brand Vision.It is important to create a strong platform upon which the brand will be built. A good brand vision will involve articulating the kind of brand you want to build, including character and personality of the brand. If the brand were a human being, what characteristics and personality would he have? Personality and character will determine appearance. Will your brand be youthful and adventurous, or understated and conservative? You must be able to define personality and character for your brand, so that your designers will get a good brief for what the appearance or more appropriately, visual identity would look like. It's like conceiving and giving birth to a child before naming and clothing the child. Before you choose color and clothing, you would at least have determined the sex of the child.

There are 3 steps to creating a strong identity.

1. Develop a compelling value proposition
2. Define personality and character for the brand
3. Design logo and visual identity that project that personality and character

4. Develop sensual aspects of identity and other dimensions of brand behavior which will reinforce your value proposition

More importantly, it is necessary to work with professionals in this process. The days of "my 12 year old did that logo for me" are days of ignorance!

THE FIFTH DIMENSION

"

Once you have articulated a brand promise, everything you say or do must reinforce that promise. Unfortunately, this rarely happens because most companies promise what they cannot deliver, while others promise different things at different times and never keep any of those promises.

"

BRAND BEHAVIOR

WHAT IS BRAND BEHAVIOR?

When you consider that brands are very much like human beings, it becomes easier to understand the concept of brand behavior. A brand is a bundle of promises. The process of brand management therefore must revolve around the consistent and sustainable fulfillment of those promises. However when a brand fails to live up to its promises, it will not achieve the trust and loyalty of customers. Loyalty is what results in repeat patronage as well as word of mouth promotion. So where there is no brand loyalty, growth is stunted. The most fundamental function of the brand manager is to ensure that brand behavior aligns with brand promise.

For most brands, the challenge is about living up to promises made. Competitive pressures often make companies promise what they cannot deliver in a sustainable way. As highlighted in The Second Dimension, value proposition must be unique, desirable and deliverable. Even when these criteria are met, there must be a deliberate strategy to ensure the brand always lives up to that promise.

DIMENSIONS OF BRAND BEHAVIOR

In 2004, USP developed a template to help organizations improve on brand behavior. The template helps in the implementation of the company's Integrated Brand Marketing Strategy, IBMS. It highlights the various ways in which a typical corporate brand acts, and shows the relationship between those brand actions and the core brand promise or value proposition. When brand actions are driven by a single minded value proposition, two things happen. One is the effective establishment of a strong positioning and perception. The other is the brand's ability to consistently deliver on its promise. It is on this dual premise that strong and successful brands are built.

IBMS-Building A Synergy

*   *USP's Integrated Brand Marketing Template*

The Brand Promise or Brand Value Proposition should be at the centre of everything a company does. Once you have articulated a brand promise, everything you say or do must reinforce that promise. Unfortunately, this rarely happens because most companies promise what they can not deliver, while others promise different things at different times and never keep any of those promises. Having dealt extensively with brand promise in The Second Dimension, the point to note here is very simple; never promise what you can not consistently deliver.

After establishing the promise, reinforce it with everything you say or do. For most corporate brands, brand behavior may be dimensioned as follows;

VISUAL IDENTITY
INTERNAL CULTURE
MARKETING AND SALES
CORPORATE SOCIAL RESPONSIBILITY (I PREFER TO CALL IT CORPORATE SOCIAL INVESTMENT)
CUSTOMER SERVICE
BRAND COMMUNICATIONS (OR ADVERTISING)

The hallmark of successful brand management is ensuring that all these dimensions of brand behavior convey a consistent message about your brand.

VISUAL IDENTITY

This is the way your brand appears. For a corporate brand, this will involve your logo and colors, your location and the general appearance of your company and its people, including how company vehicles are painted and branded. For products, this will include packaging.

INTERNAL CULTURE

This refers to the way your employees do things, including how you work and play. How you dress to work. How you celebrate anniversaries and milestones. How colleagues relate with one another.

MARKETING AND SALES

This has to do with the way you create value and the way(s) you go about making people pay for the value you create. The kinds of product you develop and the kinds of promotional activities you deploy are also relevant here.

CORPORATE SOCIAL INVESTMENT

This is the way you appreciate your community, by giving something back. It is generally perceived as a way of behaving responsibly. Corporate brand behavior is often narrowed down to this dimension.

CUSTOMER SERVICE

This entails the kind of system or structure you have put in place to create the desired customer experience. What is the customer experience you create, and how does it reinforce your brand promise?

BRAND COMMUNICATIONS

This is the totality of everything you communicate about your brand. This extends beyond advertising which is just one form of brand communications. It involves the message you get across and the way you get it across to your target.

ALIGNING BRAND BEHAVIOR WITH BRAND PROMISE

To begin with, brand managers must align themselves with the saying; actions speak louder than words. People will judge you more by your actions than by your words. Do not be misled by the assumption that constant repetition of your brand promise is what will make people believe it as the proponents of massive advertising would have you believe. What really matters at the end of the day is the extent to which you *live the brand.*

USP carried out a survey on the banking sector in 2008, as a follow up to a similar survey done three years earlier. The survey revealed that 45% of respondents were indeed aware of their banks' brand promise compared to 9% recorded in the 2005 survey. However, only 21% agreed that their banks were living up to their brand promises while 19% said their banks were not living up to their brand promise. 5% were undecided.

15% of respondents further claimed to have held their banks accountable regarding their promises, either by withdrawing their patronage or drawing the bank's attention to its failure to live up to its promise. Generally, more than ever, people now expect companies to deliver on their promises.

While companies can easily go on management retreats and articulate value propositions, is it easy to galvanize the company's entire workforce and systems behind such value propositions? This is where the greater challenge lies.

CSR OR CSI?

Do you think of it as Corporate Social Responsibility or Corporate Social Investment? A common indicator of brand behavior is CSR. Most companies eagerly accept the need to "give back to society". However the traditional concept of "charitable donations" does not deliver optimal value in terms of increasing brand equity. While most companies appreciate the need to spend a certain amount of money every year towards expressing their corporate kindness, very few implement such activity within the concept of a centrally defined brand strategy.

The general practice is to make a budgetary provision for CSR, and spend it on charitable donations and disaster relief. A common way of getting brand mileage from such donations is the use of media coverage. A group of company executives are pictured donating food items at motherless babies' homes. The picture appears in the newspapers over the next couple of days, and that is it. This however rarely delivers any enduring value to the brand.

1. It is common practice, and therefore does not confer any form of uniqueness on the brand.
2. It is transient, and is so quickly forgotten.

When the practice of giving back to society is viewed as an investment rather than a responsibility, companies are more likely to derive greater benefits from what they give.

GETTING MORE FROM YOUR CSR

The essence of good brand behavior is to ensure that there is correlation between what a brand communicates and what it does. Since CSR is a common indicator of what people generally perceive to be responsible corporate behavior, I will dwell on how brands can effectively institute a strong CSR platform and increase brand equity.

THE INTEGRATED APPROACH

How can companies align their CSR with their brand positioning and value proposition? It is not enough for a company to simply develop a culture of giving back to society. There must be a method behind the giving. The action must make a definite statement about what the brand stands for. This will not only project a certain consistency about the brand but will also reinforce the value proposition through action, thereby increasing brand equity. When this is done, it becomes CSI.

Let us consider a hypothetical case;

EFFICO BANK is a bank that has been created for the academic community. The financial needs of students and lecturers are the main focus of this bank.

EFFICO BANK'S VISION

To create Africa's most advanced society

EFFICO BANK'S MISSION

To develop the most intellectually empowered populace in the world, by giving financial muscle to academic and intellectual pursuits

Naturally, Effico Bank will have its branches in all the universities, polytechnics and other higher institutions and secondary schools in the country. Having clearly defined its focus, its branch expansion strategy will follow this direction.

EFFICO BANK'S CSI

Given the bank's brand platform, its Corporate Social Investment must support education if it is to align with the core value proposition. For example, it may involve giving scholarships to those less able to fund their education. It may also involve funding academic research. This bank will donate books and libraries rather than foodstuff!

It is however not enough to focus CSI efforts on causes that align with your value proposition. It is more effective to adopt what I call the branded approach. In this case, EFFICO BANK may brand its CSI initiatives under a program to be known as KNOWLEDGE FUND.

THE IEI EXAMPLE

International Energy Insurance, IEI is the first insurance company in Nigeria to focus specifically on the energy sector. Now, this is surprising, considering that IEI was established in 2004 in a country that has been a major exporter of crude oil for more than four decades! This of course is due to what I refer to as "the fear of positioning". People assume that if they focus on a particular sector, they will lose the opportunities that lie in other sectors. So they try to be all things to all people!

The promoters of IEI had taken over ownership of an erstwhile moribund insurance company known as Global Assurance Limited. The company therefore needed to implement a comprehensive branding program. USP was engaged to manage the process.

IEI was positioned as a caring company whose brand essence is captured in the *Care in 3 Ways* philosophy. The company's value proposition is simply and consistently communicated. The *Care in 3 Ways* philosophy means that IEI cares about;

1. People
2. Businesses
3. The Environment

The company's CSI therefore flows from this platform to embrace pro-environment causes. A strategic partnership was promptly established with the Nigerian Conservation Foundation, NCF. And today an entire forest in the Northern Nigerian State of Kano was planted by IEI. It is critical that brand behavior fulfils brand promise, because over time, this is what builds equity for the brand and makes people trust and stay loyal to it.

There are certain peculiarities in the Nigerian culture and economy that create some challenges for brand owners in this respect. To begin with, the economy is structured in such a way that governments at state and federal levels control more than 70% of business activity. For most companies, government is the biggest client. What this means for a company is that a great deal of their CSI activities are politically motivated. Your company depends on government contracts. The First Lady is launching a healthcare initiative. You are invited to the launch ceremony. Your company makes financial commitment to that cause, regardless of whether it reinforces your brand value proposition or not. This is quite typical of companies in the financial sector, as well as civil and engineering contracting firms.
These factors notwithstanding, companies will do well to have a CSI focus which reinforces their brand promise. This should be pursued consistently, while making provision for the occasional politically motivated activity.

THE SIXTH DIMENSION

"

If more companies and their agencies could channel their creativity towards creating value, rather than attention grabbing adverts they would achieve a lot more. Unfortunately, what is prevalent is a quest for award winning adverts, rather than award winning brands.

"

BRAND COMMUNICATIONS

When we started what may be termed "the brand revolution" in Nigeria in 2002, one question I had to answer repeatedly was; what is the difference between branding and advertising? Marketing communications reporters never ceased to ask this question. As I tried to make the answer as simple as possible, I eventually came up with;

"Advertising is what you say while branding is what you do"

Why was it necessary to draw this distinction? In 2001, USP, then an award winning advertising agency, started a series of articles in *The Financial Standard* called **Marketing Brands.** The series was aimed at creating awareness on brands and branding. It sought to enlighten Nigerian businesses on ways they could better create value and gain competitive advantage in a highly competitive market. The thinking was quite straightforward. We live in a high tech age, where technology has made it difficult for anybody to claim superior quality. Most products now operate at the competitive point of parity. Our companies have to compete both locally and globally, since successive governments do not have a consistent policy on what comes in or goes out of the country.

It was also clear to us that the developed countries of the world were able to create wealth by creating globally competitive brands. Therefore, for us to be able to create wealth and eradicate poverty, not only in Nigeria but across Africa, we must begin to create globally competitive brands. We reasoned and still argue that for every bottle of Coke we consume in Nigeria, we are enriching some folks in the United States where that brand originated from. And that is just one example.

In 2003, a compilation of those articles was published as **Marketing Brands, Volume 1**. That year marked the last phase in the company's evolution from an advertising agency to a brand management consultancy. Since then the series has been published in Thisday, BusinessDay and Bottom Line Magazine, with more than 200 articles published.

In February of the same year, USP resigned its membership of the Association of Advertising Agencies of Nigeria AAAN, held a brand re launch event and announced its repositioning as Nigeria's Premier Brand Management Consultancy. Expectedly, this move angered the advertising establishment, which commenced a deliberate campaign to create the perception that branding and advertising are one and the same! Since the concept of branding as a professional practice was relatively new in the country, the advertising agencies have been able to create confusion in the minds of people. Even though, quite a number of brand consultancies later emerged, the traditional ad agencies insisted there was no distinction! This is why the question kept coming up! That confusion has been a factor in what I describe as Nigeria's peculiar culture of "wasteful advertising".

While advertising is just one component of the branding process and can not on its own achieve the objective of building a strong brand, at USP, we prefer to call this function Brand Communications, because the latter term is more effective at making the communication more brand focused and media neutral.

I have deliberately left this topic to be treated towards the end of this book for the simple reason that brand communications has its place at the later stages of the branding process. It is only after the vision has been articulated, value proposition defined, brand character defined, marketing objectives set, that brand communications can be meaningful and effective. Unfortunately, this does not seem to be the norm. More often than not, advertising focuses on "creating awareness", based on the faulty assumption that awareness alone is enough to motivate purchase.

Writing about magazine and newspaper adverts, Christine Pilch says:

Most advertisements that get any attention at all, receive only 2 – 3 seconds of it. So why do so many companies waste these precious 2 – 3 seconds with messages that are so unappealing? If people pay attention to what interests them and ignore everything else, how can you break through the clutter with a message that people care about? All you have to do is press your customers' hot buttons. People naturally resist change and when you ask them to try your product or service, you're asking them to change what they usually do. Your job is to convince people to change their habit and spend money with you, so your advertising must instantly communicate the benefits of changing their habit, thus touch their hot buttons.

You've got a huge advantage over your competition if you've taken the time to position your company after (1) learning what is important to your customers (2) determining what problem your product or service can solve for them, and (3) articulating why your company is the best or only choice. As a result of that advantage, you can now create more powerful ads.

*Ads that speak about your years in business, awards won, and promises of quality, service and lowest price may gratify your ego, but they just don't interest the very people you're spending money to reach. These folks want to instantly know what you have that benefits them.*22

Thankfully, advertising that pours companies' resources down the drain is not a peculiarly Nigerian problem! When an ad does not communicate a compelling value proposition, it is more often than not, a waste of money. The practice of ego gratifying advertising is most evident in the banking industry where banks spend millions of naira just to advertise some award they have won! A widespread inability to clearly differentiate advertising from branding is equally responsible for this waste.

If more companies and their agencies could channel their creativity towards creating value, rather than attention grabbing adverts they would achieve a lot more. Unfortunately, what is prevalent is a quest for award winning adverts, rather than award winning brands.

The HABIB NIGERIA BANK Example

In 2001, our firm was engaged to develop a positioning campaign for Habib Nigeria Bank. At that time the bank was facing stiff competition particularly from the "second generation" banks. The trend was to deploy state-of-the-art information technology towards improving customer service. Habib Bank however was a "laggard" in this regard, as most of its branches were not on line. It was an era during which most banks were boasting an "on line, real time" network. In spite of this however, the bank had its strong points. It was conservative and gave its customers personalized service.

After asking a number of fundamental questions, we realized that what customers wanted from their banks had hardly changed, and the most enduring values of banking would always be relevant. In the course of our research, we discovered that when the bank was founded 20 years earlier, the founding Chairman in an address to the pioneer staff of the bank had emphasized integrity and the traditional values of banking. Those values had, commendably been upheld by the bank since inception!

It was based on this core essence of the bank that a new positioning campaign was developed, which projected the bank as a proudly conservative bank driven by the traditional values of Trust, Integrity and Security. Before then, banks and their creative agencies had created the perception that conservatism was negative and a bank had to be "dynamic" and had to be "changing with the times". Meanwhile the most essential function of a bank is the conservation of wealth and the guarantee of security. One would think it is obvious that the word "conservatism" derives from "to conserve". I am yet to find a bank customer that does not expect his bank to "conserve" whatever deposits he puts there!

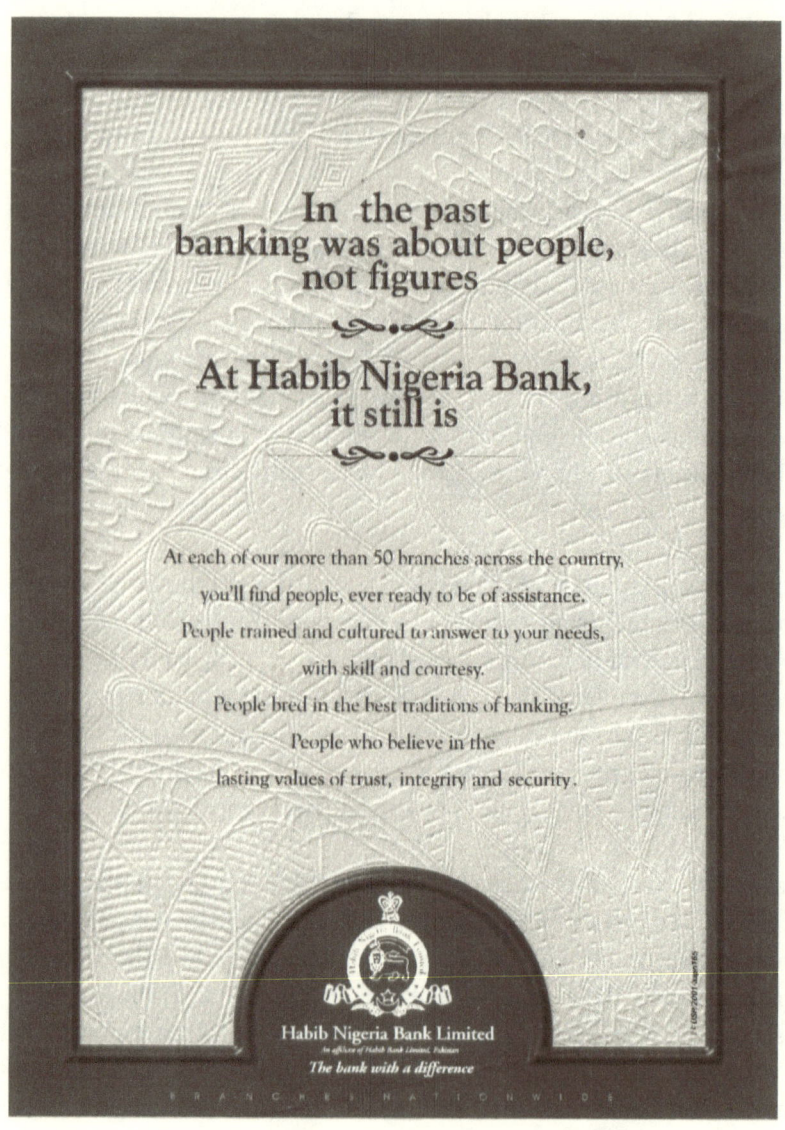

*   *One of Habib Bank's ads, expressing the bank's conservative positioning*

During my days in advertising agencies, there was always that debate on what is creative and what is not. It was commonly said that an ad that does not sell is not creative. This assertion is based on the premise that the most important function of an ad is to sell a product or service. This premise is faulty, but the advertising establishment, stuck five decades behind, would never agree. What sells a product is not the adverts, but what that product offers. You would ask a client; what makes your product unique? And he would say: it's just like any other product in its category. You guys are the experts and you should be able to create adverts that will make it look unique. So the ad agency guys come up with "creative" concepts. The client runs the ads for months without seeing the impact he expects. At the end of the year, he sacks the agency and calls for proposals from other agencies. He wants "fresh ideas" and a more "creative" agency! It's an all too familiar cycle.

In the early 90s, there existed an ad agency by the name M C & A. In its heyday, it was one of the frontline agencies in the country and implemented a number of memorable ad campaigns. One of those campaigns was for CTMC, a mortgage finance company. Two decades later, a lot of people still remember the radio jingle with the refrain: *CTMC, I de your hand ooo!* Of course, it was an award winning campaign. But both ad agency and CTMC have since folded up.

One of the second generation banks in the country was Fortune Bank. It had an award winning outdoor campaign for one of its products called The Fortune Green Account. While there was an award for the "creativity" of the advert, we were not told how many customers took up the product based on their exposure to that advert. The bank had since been acquired by United Bank for Africa.

More recently, when most companies claimed to be "branding" while actually running wasteful advertising campaigns, we have had award winning adverts that only succeeded in magnifying the company's limited understanding of the branding process. A good example ironically is Bank PHB, which emerged from the forced merger of Platinum Bank and Habib Bank during the consolidation era.

THE BANK PHB EXPERIENCE

Following the merger in 2005, the newly formed Bank PHB resolved to position itself "as an innovative, brilliant/creative institution". According to the CEO Francis Atuche, this required "the mutation of most of the internal processes". The bank sought to achieve differentiation through a branding program. It adopted a naming strategy which helped in achieving this objective. It chose to be called BANK PHB, rather than the predictable PHB BANK.

After developing a new visual identity, the bank launched an aggressive communication campaign. Created by one of the leading ad agencies in the country, the campaign received wide acclaim, and expectedly won an award. In an attempt to position the bank as "futuristic", one of the ad proclaims; ONE DAY, CARS WILL RUN ON WATER. Another one says; ONE DAY, CARS WILL DRIVE THEMSELVES. The ads claim that the bank was already thinking in this way.

What does this offer me as a customer? Does it mean if I had a revolutionary idea, I could take it to this bank for funding? Does it mean the bank would support research that sought to break new grounds? I eventually got a good opportunity to ask these questions at a seminar at which both I and the bank's CEO were speakers. I wanted to know if the bank had actually restructured its internal processes to substantiate and give credibility to this claim. Did the bank fundamentally alter its loan approval procedure? Did it put in place a system fundamentally different from the conventional way a bank would normally appraise the viability of business plans?

Considering that most revolutionary ideas that changed the world seemed silly or sounded crazy at first, did the bank entrench a uniquely and fundamentally different risk management philosophy? If I had a proposal for the invention of the world's first water-powered automotive engine, would the bank fund it? If I had a plan to build a theme park on the moon, would the bank fund it?

His answer;

It's difficult, because the risk management people always tell you we can't do this.

Now, why create the perception that you could do what you know your risk management people would never let you do?

Says the CEO " If branding is the holistic way a company is managed, then the safest way to creating the best brands is to ensure your people are treated in a manner to make them perceive the organization in the same way you want to be perceived by the public. If your people are ever doubtful, cynical or resentful to the brand, it's very likely only your consultants and advertisers will gain from the brand building process and your bottom line will be the worse for it." This is what eventually happened to Bank PHB!

Here was a bank that had invested billions of naira on a positioning platform that was neither credible nor deliverable and a "creative" award winning campaign. Less than three years into this audacious and bold campaign, Bank PHB was in trouble. It was listed among the five distressed banks in the country, and the CEO and executive management were sacked by the Central Bank of Nigeria.

THE STORY OF INTERCONTINENTAL BANK PLC

While Intercontinental Bank suffered a similar fate, it had a different and perhaps a more unfortunate story. Bank PHB was attempting to develop a new brand. However Intercontinental Bank was already a strong brand which was destroyed in what the management of the bank thought was a branding program.

The bank was established in 1989 as Nigerian Intercontinental Merchant Bank Limited, and focused on wholesale banking. Its CEO Erastus Akingbola was a product of the old school and instituted a culture of conservatism and integrity. Within ten years, the bank had built a strong balance sheet and a sterling reputation for reliability. It remained solid while other banks its age faltered. It had some of the most patronized investment products in the industry including the Intercontinental Diamond Fund, IDF.

With the introduction of universal banking, which allowed merchant banks to change their operating licenses and engage in retail banking, Intercontinental Bank became the first to switch. This was however carefully managed with little alteration to the bank's visual identity. With the consolidation program and the need for banks to increase their capital base to a minimum of 25 Billion Naira, the bank had a unique edge by way of controlling stakes in three other banks. The formal acquisition of those banks was virtually hitch-free and the bank did not have to change its name.

Unfortunately, the bank became a victim of the unhealthy competition that followed the consolidation program. Suddenly, survival was now a matter of size, or so the banks believed. To reposition for global competitiveness, the bank engaged in a "re branding" that resulted in a radical transformation of its visual identity.

Having worked closely with the bank over a ten-year period I know some of the tough internal arguments that the visual identity review generated. With the core of its pioneer executive management still in place, any suggestion to change the bank's logo was often fiercely resisted. More than five years earlier, USP had advised the bank on the need to review its logo and identity and "shed some weight" without losing its core essence. This idea was rejected. The CEO's argument was that while the bank needed to be "repositioned", it did not need to "re brand". He then likened the bank to a young village girl that needed to be taken to one of the world's big cities, like New York. That response highlighted the confusion that branding had already generated in the country.

When several years later the bank decided to review its visual identity, it went to the extreme. In its quest to be "more visible", it created a loud image that undermined its core essence of conservatism and created branches which according to one newspaper columnist looked like "candy shops". Years earlier, the bank had undergone three changes to its visual identity, all managed by USP. None was radical. The first change was its transition from merchant banking to universal banking. All we did was remove "Merchant" from the bank's name. The second change was carried out when the bank became a public limited company. The typeface was softened, and "Limited" was replaced with "Plc". These changes were so minimal they hardly fundamentally affected people's perception of the bank. Lastly, when the bank acquired three other banks during the consolidation program, the "weight shedding" was finally done, and the bank was generally perceived to have had the most seamless integration, a robust capital base and sound fundamentals.

Then the bank decided to join the band wagon of those seeking "branding experts" from South Africa. Suddenly, the bank wanted to be more visible. A new identity was created and a huge campaign followed. Several billions of Naira was expended on ego gratifying advertising to create the perception of a "global brand" including advertising space at the newly opened Heathrow Terminal 5. Two years later, Intercontinental Bank was in trouble. A Central Bank of Nigeria audit revealed the bank was bankrupt. The CEO was sacked, and its entire Board was dissolved. The bank had wrongly assumed that you could use advertising to create a brand that didn't exist!

How could top management people, with decades of experience plus local and international training at some of the world's best business schools make these faulty and costly assumptions about branding? Part of the answer lies in the way the corporate communication function was being handled in the banks. Many banks recruited journalists from the media houses to handle this function, with focus on what gets published about the banks in the news media. Many of them were either called "Head, Corporate Affairs" or "Head, Corporate Communications".

After USP repositioned as Nigeria's Premier Brand Management Consultancy, and started championing the branding crusade in Nigeria, many companies began to embrace the branding process. These heads of corporate affairs and corporate communications gradually began to call themselves "Head of Brand Management", with no marketing training or experience! Yet their CEO's did not see what was wrong with this grand deception. With these people coordinating the branding process in the banks, there were bound to be problems along the way.

THE BEST ADVERTISING IS THE TRUTH

It does not matter how attractive your advert layout is, or how elegant the graphics are. If the advert does not contain a compelling value proposition, it's a waste of money. Worse still, if it raises expectation for what you can not deliver, this is even worse. I once sat in the office of a senior executive of Bank PHB, who told me that their branding had been so successful that the only challenge they now had was trying to live up to the expectation of their customers! He said the brand was ahead of them, and they were racing to catch up with it!

The real great challenge is for companies to create compelling truths about their brands, and communicate those truths in their advertising. Ever so often, we see companies putting the cart before the horse. Does it make sense to create attractive claims, and now struggle to live up to it?

When we were engaged to help Guardian Express Bank (which later became a part of the Spring Bank Group) in its recapitalization program, there was no option to the simple truth. Here was a four-year-old bank, which had little to boast of in an era when other banks were advertising the handsome returns they had delivered to their shareholders over the years. The bank came out with the simple truth, running ads that say; WE WONT PROMISE YOU THE EARTH.

The campaign focused on the modest truth about the bank, and encouraged the investing public to share its vision of making banking a simple, less complicated experience for its customers.

It worked. The bank attracted more investment than the target set for its management! Nothing works better than the simple verifiable truth. When companies succumb to competitive pressure and promise what they can not deliver they forget that people are not necessarily expecting you to move the earth. A simple promise you can deliver is far stronger than a big promise you can not keep.

THE SEVENTH DIMENSION

"

Our nation branding efforts must recognize the difference between branding and advertising. This is the kind of thinking that builds great brands. We cannot become great by saying it. We have to do great things!

"

BRAND ECONOMICS

The examples cited in the last chapter of failed branding programs underlie a more fundamental problem with our economy and how a better understanding of the economics of branding can help us create wealth by creating value. The problems that befell the banks in question led to massive job losses. This however is only a part of the story. The other part is that while the banks were claiming superficial growth, there was very little for them to grow on. Bank PHB's CEO once challenged people to "check the growth in Bank PHB shares over the past nine months", as proof of how successful the bank's branding program had been. A year later, the share value had plummeted to less than 5% of what it once had been!

Shortly after the consolidation, a number of Nigerian Banks tried to position themselves as "global" brands. They seemed to have wholeheartedly embraced the branding process, and had raised customer service standards to internationally acceptable levels. In spite of the challenges of weak infrastructure and epileptic power supply, they had built on-line real-time branch networks and had deployed ATMs. While some had become globally competitive, none had achieved the status of a global brand. But this is what was being proclaimed in their adverts! Having a few branches outside of the country does not make you a "global" brand. While the claim may reflect your vision and ambition, it overstates your status and implies a lack of understanding of what "global" means, within the context of brands and branding.

A couple of Nigerian banks were listed among the world's top 1000 banks, including Intercontinental Bank. At that point it appeared we were in the process of building globally competitive brands in the financial sector. This could prepare the ground and the basis for positioning the country as Africa's Financial Centre. I brought up this scenario during my interview with the CEO of Skye Bank, Akinsola Akinfemiwa. His remarks were quite instructive. To him, you can only build a global brand if certain conditions in your operating environment are right. By this token, a bank could become a global brand if it has the local economy to grow on.

Given the strategic role banks have to play especially in a developing economy, the symbiosis that must exist between the banks and the economy would mean that the banks help the economy grow and as the economy grows it grows the banks' balance sheet. This can now fuel the growth and expansion that would take the brand to other parts of the world. An African proverb says you must stand firmly in your own compound, before you can stretch your neck to look into other people's compounds!

The Nigerian story is unique. While the banks were yearly declaring huge profits, other sectors of the economy, especially the critical manufacturing sector was groaning. Their problems include weak infrastructure, poor power supply and unavailability of credit. So what economy were the banks growing on? By the time some of them were declared insolvent their single largest debtor was a stockbroker who employed less than 20 people! In a country of over 150 million people, with vast oil and gas wealth, the single largest bank debtor employed less than 20 people, and owed almost $1Billion. In order to fuel the kind of growth that would justify their wild claims, the banks had to resort to stock market speculation as a short cut to huge profits. The nature of banking dictates that you can not grow bigger than the economy in which you operate, but you can grow the economy. Growing the economy is a longer term, more painstaking approach which the banks would rather not adopt.

The banks often cite frequent policy changes of Government as a factor that increases credit risk. Imagine funding a textile manufacturing factory, based on the fact that textile imports have been banned, only for the ban to be lifted after a year or two! This means our understanding of the economics of branding must begin at the very top. But before we go to the top, let

116

us consider the banks, who in recent times appear to be the champions of "branding". Several of these banks, including Intercontinental Bank and Bank PHB engaged the services of foreign brand consultants. Their position was that the foreigners were the "experts" and had more experience in branding since they had practiced it for much longer. If that was the case why did the CEOs retain their positions instead of employing Europeans who had more "experience" in banking?

This position betrays a naked ignorance of the economics of branding. A bank outsources services it could obtain locally to a foreign company that does not employ its citizens and does not pay tax in its country, depriving its own customers of the patronage they so badly need, in order to generate employment and increase their patronage of these same banks! How can these banks thrive and become global brands?

I once asked the former Chairman of the Board of one of these banks and ironically a renowned economist and one time Presidential aspirant, why his bank engaged foreign brand consultants. His answer was that in a free market economy, you could go anywhere you like, to get the best service possible. Given the eminent position of this man among the nation's intellectual elite, his response made me shudder at the nation's bleak prospects!

On a South African Airways flight from Johannesburg in April 2002, I had just finished a serving of that country's own brand of cream liqueur, Amarula. I called an air hostess and told her I wanted more Amarula. Her face lit up with a smile and she commended me for asking for it by its name! As that country hosted the 2010 World Cup, Nigeria continued to pump millions of dollars annually into her economy for products and services that could be provided by Nigerians!

"RE BRANDING" NIGERIA

The nation's advertising body once moved its annual congress to Abuja, with the theme centered on "Brand Nigeria". The "Brand Nigeria" initiative was originally championed by Akin Adeoya, then publisher of BRANDS & PRODUCTS Magazine, now Publisher of M2 Magazine. It was therefore not an idea that originated from the advertising body whose strategy is to position in such a way that it will play a major role in any effort to brand or re brand (as they call it) Nigeria.

The 22-Member Committee which the Ministry set up had at least two of the nation's best brains in advertising on it, including the President of The Advertising Agencies Association of Nigeria, AAAN. But not a single brand consultant!

To begin with, the advertising body is dominated by "affiliates". By this I mean agencies which are affiliated to foreign "global" agency networks. They wear the badges of these foreign agencies as a way of showing that they are an agency of international quality. If you are not affiliated to a foreign agency, you are not considered successful. Sadly most big spending clients would only patronize these affiliates. The top 10 advertising agencies in this country are affiliated to foreign agencies. This means they answer to some colonial masters in South Africa, Europe or North America. This means they can not pursue growth and expansion in a way that may conflict with the "brand values and identity" of the brands to which they are affiliated. It means they earn a living by promoting foreign brands.

Some of them even drop their original names and adopt the names of their foreign principals. They will tell you in their presentations that they belong to a global network "with offices in over 200 countries". These global networks exist today, because some people had the vision to establish and nurture them. And as it so often happens, some guys in North America will wake up one day and pay a couple billions of dollars to buy the foreign agency, simply because it is present in hundreds of countries and is truly a global brand. Now who is smarter? Is it the guys that created the brand or those who wear the badge and blindly embrace economic colonialism?

On the Nation Branding level, the economics of the process remain barely understood! And if we look at the very nature of the way our top advertising agencies operate, they negate the very essence of branding and should be the last anyone should consider for developing a branding program for the country. There is something deeply philosophical about branding that goes beyond the theories many of us read in books. Yet it is simply a matter of common sense!

Branding is the greatest wealth creator in the world today. The rich nations are rich because they have created and built global brands which they have successfully sold to the rest of the world. For every Yamaha generator or motorcycle we see around us, Japan is the richer for it. And for every Nokia handset we switch on, a tiny European country named Finland is the richer for it. Even though Africa is blessed with enormous natural resources, Africans have remained poor because we are not building globally competitive brands. China has become an economic superpower in the world today, because "Made in China" no longer means "inferior".

Creating globally competitive brands is not limited to products. You can create a globally competitive tourism brand. This is what the United Arab Emirates has done successfully with Dubai. Our people are poor today because we are not creating globally competitive brands, which would create millions of jobs and transform lives. As a brand, a nation needs to become globally competitive.

In Nigeria's Federal Capital Territory, the best hotels are foreign brands! Top on the list of course is the Transcorp Hilton, which is well patronized by the Federal Government. They spend billions annually of our tax payers' money, promoting and sustaining this foreign brand! Yet in far away America, a certain young girl whose name is Paris Hilton will never be poor in her life, simply because her name is Hilton, and she is grand daughter of the man who created this hotel brand! And guess where our nation's advertising body held its Brand Nigeria Congress? The Hilton of course!

Nigeria once had a couple of good hotel brands. But rather than develop them into global brands, they were given away to foreigners. Ikoyi Hotel was re opened as Southern Sun, a South African brand. Durbar Hotel, which was re named Golden Tulip. The company that has pumped billions of naira into this renovation and the promotion of the Golden Tulip brand is none other than one of our conglomerates, UAC, whose pay off line is "doing good".

Now let us consider PROTEA HOTEL, a South African brand which has suddenly sprung up all over Nigeria. The South Africans simply came with their brand. They have wisely concentrated on building a brand, while Nigerians are busy building hotels. If you go to their website, they will tell you how many Protea Hotels there are across Africa, including Nigeria. Who is the smarter here? A hotel is mere brick and glass. A brand is far much more!

For our country to be a globally competitive brand, it must meet a certain minimum internationally acceptable standard of development. This means uninterrupted power supply, world class airports, excellent educational institutions, social security, social infrastructure, low unemployment level, a minimum standard of living that guarantees decent housing and other basic comforts. The average Nigerian is a microcosm of the Nation Brand, and we must be committed to uplifting the standard of living of the average Nigerian.

But this is only the minimum. For us to be a great nation brand, we must begin to do great things. Our thinking must follow this direction; WE ARE THE BIGGEST BLACK NATION IN THE WORLD, WE MUST BUILD THE BIGGEST AIRPORT IN AFRICA; AS ONE OF THE LARGEST OIL PRODUCERS IN THE WORLD, WE MUST BUILD THE WORLD'S LARGEST PETROCHEMICAL INDUSTRY; AS THE BIGGEST BLACK NATION IN THE WORLD, WE DESERVE TO HAVE THE BIGGEST HOTEL IN AFRICA, THE TALLEST BUILDING IN AFRICA MUST BE FOUND IN OUR COUNTRY, THE BIGGEST STADIUM, THE BIGGEST AND BEST HOSPITAL, THE BIGGEST LEISURE RESORT MUST BE FOUND ON OUR SHORES, THE BIGGEST AND BEST UNIVERSITY IN AFRICA MUST BELONG TO US.

Our nation branding efforts must recognize the difference between branding and advertising. This is the kind of thinking that builds great brands. We can not become great by saying it. We have to do great things!

References

1. Brand Positioning and Brand Creation, Anne Bahr Thompson, Brands And Branding (The Economist), 2003. ibid.
2. Built To Last, Jim Collins & Jerry I. Porras, 2005. pg 220
3. www.ubaplc.com
4. Built To Last, Jim Collins & Jerry Porras, 2005. pg 50 ibid ibid. pg 46 ibid.
5. Managing Markets, Segments, and Customers, by Das Narayandas
6. Source: Middle East & Africa Wireless Analyst, July 5 2006.
7. Foreword to *Positioning,* Al Ries and Jack Trout. 2001.
8. Positioning, Al Ries and Jack Trout, 2001. Pg 2 ibid.
9. Brands & Brands, The Economist, 2003. Pg 2 ibid.
10. Perceptual Mapping, Populus
11. Corporate Identity, Wally Olins, 1999, pg 7. ibid.
12. Logos, by Conway Lloyd Morgan, 1999. Pg 15
13. Jared McCarthy, MarketingProfs, 2007
14. Ibid.
15. Christine Pilch, Marketing Profs, September 5, 2006

www.ingramcontent.com/pod-product-compliance
Lightning Source LLC
Chambersburg PA
CBHW020303290526
45784CB00003B/1344